Splendid Audacity

The Story of Pacific University

Splendid Audacity
The Story of Pacific University

BY

GARY MIRANDA

AND

RICK READ

PRODUCED BY

DOCUMENTARY BOOK PUBLISHERS

SEATTLE, WASHINGTON

Splendid Audacity
The Story of Pacific University

© 2000 PACIFIC UNIVERSITY

Pacific University, 2043 College Way, Forest Grove, OR 97116
503-357-6151

Authors: Gary Miranda and Rick Read
Project Manager: Dr. Christopher Wilkes
Cover and book design: Susan Blettel
Copy Editors: Sandy Marvinney, Gabrielle Byrd-Williams
Publisher: Pacific University
Printed in Hong Kong

Miranda, Gary
    Splendid Audacity: The Story of Pacific University/text by Gary Miranda and Rick Read
    p.cm.
    Includes bibliographical references and index
    ISBN 0-935503-30-7
    1. Pacific University — History I. Read, Rick 1953-   II. Title
99-053530

Produced by Documentary Book Publishers, 615 Second Avenue, Suite 260, Seattle, WA 98104
206-467-4300; E-mail: docbooks@SasquatchBooks.com
www.sasquatchbooks.com
Documentary Book Publishers publishes books for corporate and institutional clients across North America.

PHOTOGRAPHS

All photographs used are from the Pacific University Archives or other Pacific University collections unless otherwise noted in the photograph credits at the back of the book.

Contents

President's Foreword

Faith Gabelnick

Splendid Audacity, The Story of Pacific University draws us into the fabric of American history and the stories of the dreamers, pioneers, and visionaries who believed in preparing students to serve their changing society. Reading this story, we learn that Pacific University is linked through the founding Congregationalists to other significant colleges and universities in the United States, and to their legacy of excellence in liberal arts education.

Through the years, Pacific has been able to shape and focus its identity to include, within its core liberal arts heritage, the additional responsibility of preparing graduate professionals to work in the fields of health and education. Now, at the edge of the millennium, Pacific is a comprehensive university of almost 2,000 students, thriving as a connected and sustaining community.

The story of Pacific as researched and interpreted by our authors, Gary Miranda and Rick Read, demonstrates how Pacific maintained a sense of vigor and optimism despite many daunting challenges, and shows how it has gradually achieved a new level of maturity and self-confidence that will carry it through the next periods of transformation.

Our vision for the next years is expressed in our Strategic Plan 2004, which asserts that Pacific University "will be recognized nationally for its exemplary undergraduate programs that focus specifically on connecting the liberal arts with practical professional preparation, and for its outstanding graduate programs in health sciences and education."

Splendid Audacity shows us how fortunate we are now, as in the past, to have the essential ingredients to carry us forward to accomplish this vision — we have gifted and dedicated staff and managers, an intelligent and creative student body, and excellent faculty who come together as a community to meet our challenges. Our university community is complex and vigorous — ever youthful in its optimism and energy, yet seasoned by challenges, disappointments, and hard-won achievements.

We understand from reading this wonderful book that our institution's identity is a patchwork of dreams and ideas, stitched together by reflection and held in our memories over the generations. How appropriate that as a part of the sesquicentennial preparations, a dozen women on campus made a quilt to recognize Pacific's history. These women met every day for almost a year to design and create this quilt. As they sat together and talked, they, like their predecessors and the historians, pieced together patches of history, threads of

Pacific University's commemorative sesquicentennial quilt

their souls. The quilt is a wonderful metaphor, both as an historical artifact and as a story, for the spirit and reality, the theory and the practice, of living in community at Pacific.

Like its pioneering founders, Pacific is reaching today beyond its local boundaries to stay connected with its alumni, its friends and supporters, its faculty and staff. Partnerships with public school systems, with foundations, and with corporations are part of Pacific's new story, as is its enhanced ambition to be a regionally and nationally distinctive, comprehensive university.

As we embark on our next 150 years, *Splendid Audacity* reminds us to honor our past. 150 years is a long legacy in the Pacific Northwest, but as we continue to create new programs and envision others, it is clear that we are still vigorous, generative, and fully alive to new possibilities. In looking forward, I am struck by how fortunate we are to be a connected and sustaining community capable of audaciously splendid acts.

Faith Gabelnick

FAITH GABELNICK
President

7

Acknowledgments

When I was invited by members of the Sesquicentennial Committee to write the history of Pacific University, I was both pleased and perplexed. Pleased that they thought I could do it; perplexed that they should ask me to do it when they might have asked a scholar or an historian — or, at the very least, an alumnus. I am none of these. Insofar as my credentials as a writer bear on the matter at all, I am a poet, a claim that will establish about as much authority in the present context as if I had declared that I am a Sagittarian.

Having completed the task for which I was chosen, I find the choice no less improbable but far less perplexing. To have made a more probable choice, in fact, would have been out of character, since Pacific has an established history of favoring the long odds. Tualatin Academy and Pacific University were founded by people for whom the only difference between the difficult and the impossible was that the impossible might take longer. All of this is reflected in the phrase, "acts of splendid audacity," which was used by one of Pacific's earliest chroniclers to describe its founding. Whether Pacific's choice of its latest chronicler was as splendid as it was audacious, I must leave to the readers to decide.

Which is not to suggest that I produced this book single-handedly. Any such effort is necessarily the work of many hands and minds, and the present book is no exception. Allow me to acknowledge some of these.

First of all, I must acknowledge and thank my co-author and former archivist of Pacific University, Rick Read. Without Rick, the book you are reading would not have been possible — which is to say, it would have taken longer. Rick supplied much of the raw material, selected many of the photographs, provided preliminary sketches of key figures, wrote most of the sidebars, and painstakingly initiated me into the arcane mysteries of the archive filing system. He also reviewed and corrected successive drafts with the scrutiny of — well, of an archivist. In this last activity, our working relationship reminded me of the movie "Babe," in which I played the porcine lead to Rick's role as the benevolent overseer: with Rick's high standards of scholarship ever before me, I would scamper to corral the sheepish facts into their proper contexts and then wait with Babe-like docility for Rick's approving, "That will do." While I must accept both credit and blame for the voice that emerges from the narrative, Rick's invaluable contributions to the present history have more than earned him the title of "co-author."

My thanks to President Faith Gabelnick and the Pacific Sesquicentennial Committee for inviting me to tell the story of Pacific University and especially for having the good grace to let me tell it as honestly as I could. The Committee includes, in addition to President

Gabelnick: Mindy Cameron '65 and Bill Turner '63 (co-chairpersons), Tabitha Becker '84, Alma Brown, Doris Burlingham, Lois Ebel, Charlotte Filer, Alice Hoskins '56, Barbara Klein, Larry Lipin, Tim O'Malley, Rev. Rich Osburn, Fred Scheller '43, '54, Judy Sherman, Tom Sloan, Barbara Strain '70, and Chris Wilkes.

Among these, a very special thanks to Chris Wilkes, director of corporate relations and my main contact at Pacific, whose urbanity and graciousness have been a constant delight. Chris' unfailing support and encouragement over the past two years have left me with only two grounds for regret: that our monthly meetings at Borders Books will be no more, and that I will never have a British accent.

Susan Blettel deserves special mention and thanks for designing and executing the layout of the book, while continuing to fufill her many and demanding duties as manager of publications. The book project was conceived from the beginning as one in which the images would not merely accompany but complete the narrative, much as music completes the lyrics. Knowing that Susan was at her keyboard ready to work her magic on the delivered text greatly lightened my concern about its shortcomings.

A number of people already mentioned reviewed the manuscript and offered valuable suggestions. Larry Lipin, associate professor of history, was especially helpful in noting gaps and in supplying background on Congregationalism in the nineteenth century. Reverend Donald Sevetson, former Pacific University board member, devoted an entire afternoon to guiding me through the labyrinth of early missionary organizations. Others generously submitted to phone or in-person interviews with great patience, among whom are Christine Didway, Judy Sherman, Miller Ritchie, Ken Schumann, Doris Burlingham, Chuck Bafaro, Mike Clock, Gabrielle Byrd-Williams, Beth Woodward, Russ Dondero, Tom Beck, Kazuko Ikeda, Joe Story, Jim Currie, Susan Cabello, Charlotte Filer, Steve Sechrist, Tim O'Malley, and others whom I am probably forgetting. Forest Grove City Recorder/Archivist Cathy Jansen and Whitman College Archivist Larry Dodd provided assistance, David Morelli helped with research on the picayune coin, and Merrill Johnson (George Fox University) lent us the original buttons from an Indian Training School uniform.

Among the several current students of Pacific University who contributed to the project in various ways, I must single out Julie Holcomb '99, who did yeoman's work in organizing the archive material and tracking down information that was either missing or well concealed.

I want also to thank the many alumni—too many to mention by name—whom I had the opportunity to meet and chat with on various occasions, including one reunion. The almost tangible affection that these former students had for Pacific University was a constant reminder to me that the task I had been given was much more than a writing assignment; it was a sacred trust. In light of that fact, I feel compelled to offer a final note, one that touches on the matter of scale.

To tell the story of the Battle of Gettysburg in a book devoted exclusively to that event is a very different matter from dealing with that same topic in a book about the Civil War or, again, in a book on the history of the United States. All three accounts may be accurate, but as the scale of the enterprise broadens, the Battle of Gettysburg is bound to become less recognizable to those who lived through it.

Similarly, alumni from Pacific University may feel that the present history, which relies heavily on the broad strokes of presidential administrations, fails to capture the sense of what it was like to be at Pacific during a given period in time. This is regrettable but also unavoidable in sketching the history of an institution as old as Pacific University. As noted above, it is also why the Sesquicentennial Committee decided to enrich the broth of the narrative with generous portions of photographs and sidebars. The combined flavor, we hope, will satisfy the hunger for new knowledge even as it revives old memories of life at Pacific.

Bon appetit!

GARY MIRANDA

Gary Miranda

Rick Read

ACT I

The House that Marsh Built

1840s - 1890

Clearing the Ground: Harvey Clark and Tabitha Brown

So many motives exist in the minds of missionaries for saying great and good things concerning their labors, and prospects, that it is difficult to know the whole truth. Perhaps only two classes of missionaries can be found. One says too much and one not enough. — REV. HARVEY CLARK, 1844

The whole of Oregon is delightful, especially the plains, of which there are many. But this West Tualatin is the most beautiful of all. — TABITHA MOFFATT BROWN, 1847

WEST TUALATIN PLAINS, or what is now Forest Grove, may have been beautiful when Tabitha Brown made the above observation, but in 1847 neither she nor anyone else envisioned it as a site for a university. In a sense, Pacific University was not envisioned at all; it happened, like those improbable flowers that burst unbeckoned through miserly cracks in the concrete of old sidewalks. As late as September 1847, just a year before the board of trustees for Tualatin Academy was formed, the three people now officially recognized as the school's "founders" were total strangers to one another, and two of them—Reverend Harvey Clark and Tabitha Moffatt Brown—had no intention of starting a college preparatory school, let alone a college. How all of this changed in the short span of a year is where the story of Pacific University begins.

UNLIKELY FORCES

OREGON CITY, April 6, 1848.
To Stephen Prentiss, Esq., and Mrs. Prentiss, the Father and Mother of the late Mrs. Whitman of the Oregon Mission.

My Dear Father and Mother in Christ:
 Through the wonderful interposition of God in delivering me from the hand of the murderer, it has become my painful duty to apprise you of the death of your beloved daughter, Narcissa, and her worthy and appreciated husband, your honored son-in-law, Dr. Whitman. ... They were inhumanly butchered by their own, up to the last moment, beloved Indians, for whom their warm Christian hearts had prayed for eleven years, and their unwearied hands had administered to their every want in sickness and in distress. ...
 The massacre took place on the fatal

29th of November last [1847], commencing at half past one. Fourteen persons were murdered first and last. Nine men the first day. Five men escaped from the Station, three in a most wonderful manner, one of whom was the trembling writer, with whom I know you will unite in praising God for delivering even one. ...
 The Lord has transferred us from one field of labor to another. Through the kindness of Rev. Mr. Clark ... we have been brought to this place, "Tualatin Plains."
 ...Yours in deep water of affliction,

H. H. Spalding

The event to which Rev. Henry Spalding refers above is, of course, what has come to be known as "The Whitman Massacre." Why the story of Pacific University begins here will become clear soon enough, but the incident it-

Henry Harmon Spalding with the "Bible and the hoe."

The site of the Whitman Mission today. The Nez Perce name for the mission, founded in 1836, was Wailatpu — place of the rye grass.

Cushing Eells, the founder of Whitman College, was among the surviving missionaries who took refuge in the "Tualatin Plains."

self merits at least a passing commentary.

Spalding, a Presbyterian, and many of his Protestant brethren laid the blame for the "massacre" at Wailatpu (Walla Walla) on the Jesuit missionaries, who, in their view, had stirred up the Cayuse Indians to attack their alleged benefactors. The Cayuse themselves saw the situation differently: Marcus Whitman, a doctor, had spent most of the previous fall trying in vain to control a measles epidemic that ravaged the Cayuse tribe. In the two months prior to the killings, nearly half of the Cayuse population had died, including several children of their principal chief. Ugly rumors had begun to spread that Dr. Whitman was poisoning his "beloved Indians." At the very least, he was not succeeding in curing them, and Cayuse law required that bad medicine men be put to death.

Finally, there was simply the matter of what we might today call "interpersonal relations." Even in the above letter to the Prentisses announcing the death of their daughter, Spalding's salutation to the "Mother and Father of *the late Mrs. Whitman*"—coupled with his opening salvo to the "wonderful interposition of God" in delivering himself from their daughter's fate—reflects a certain lack of sensitivity that was, unfortunately, not uncommon among Spalding and his colleagues in their dealings with people in general, and with Native Americans in particular.

Whatever triggered the tragic events of November 29, 1847, it was a turning point in Pacific Northwest history. After the "massacre," angry and frightened White settlers clamored for the posting of federal troops to the region and demanded recognition of the Northwest as a U.S. territory. Ensuing battles led to treaties that stripped the Cayuse and other tribes of much of their land and confined them to reservations.

A more immediate—and for the present story, more relevant—outcome of the Whitman Massacre was that the surviving missionaries in what is now eastern Washington and western Idaho were forced to remove themselves, under military escort, to safer ground. Like Spalding and his family, they took refuge in that portion of Oregon Country called the "Tualatin Plains," an area that included present-day Forest Grove (West Tualatin Plains) and Hillsboro (East Tualatin Plains). The party included—besides Henry and Eliza Spalding—Cushing and Myra Eells, Elkanah and Mary Walker, Asa and Sarah Smith, and Alanson Hinman. All of these refugees intended to return to their missions in what would soon become the Washington Territory, but as fate and army regulations would have it, they ended up staying in the Tualatin Plains considerably longer than planned and playing various roles in the subsequent history of Pacific University. (Alanson Hinman, the only layman in the group, would stay on to become the longest-serving trustee in the history of the university.) And all of them initially depended to some degree on "the kindness of Rev. Mr. Clark," who is the more proper object of our attention.

"REV. MR. CLARK"

Harvey Clark, a native Vermonter who had been educated at Oberlin College, had arrived in the Oregon Country with his young bride, Emeline Cadwell, in 1840. Their overland journey on horseback had occurred three years before Marcus Whitman led the Great Migration Wagon Train of 1843—an exodus recog-

Harvey Clark

nized as the beginning of the westward movement along the Oregon Trail. Moreover, unlike the Whitmans, Clark had come west without official support from the American Board of Commissioners for Foreign Missions (the Oregon Country was still "foreign" at the time)—support that he had solicited and been denied.

As an independent missionary, then, Harvey Clark was something of a second-class citizen, and probably would have remained so had the Whitmans' sudden demise not landed so many prominent clergymen in his back yard. Conversely, had the newcomers—among whom was Cushing Eells, the future founder of Whitman College—not fled to the Tualatin Plains and been exposed to subsequent happenings in Forest Grove, chances are that starting an academy, and later a college, in Walla Walla would not have seemed feasible; the Whitmans, certainly, had no such intentions. Thus the Whitman Massacre played a significant part in the founding of at least two institutions of higher learning.

A Critical Vote Sets the Course for Statehood

*T*HE DRAMATIC STORY of the May 2, 1843 meeting at Champoeg, on the edge of French Prairie, is familiar to many Oregonians. Two earlier meetings had been called by the settlers in February and March of that year. They were called "Wolf Meetings" because their purpose was to discuss how to protect livestock from wolves, as well as from bears and cougars. It was during the second "Wolf Meeting" that a committee was appointed "to take into consideration the propriety of taking measures for the civil and military protection of the colony."

When 102 settlers of the northern Willamette Valley—Americans and French Canadians primarily—assembled at Champoeg to vote on their collective future under either British or American control, it shifted the balance toward U.S. occupation and set the course for statehood in 1859. Especially memorable are the decisive words of mountain man Joe Meek: "Who's for divide? All for the report of the committee and an organization, follow me!" The fact that it was such a slim majority

Harvey Clark's name is fourth from the bottom (right side) on this commemorative obelisk in Champoeg State Park.

that made the difference—with 52 voting for the provisional government and 50 voting against it—rendered the action even more legendary.

The significance of the Champoeg event is that the vote created the first government by Americans on the Pacific Coast. Coupled with the start of the Oregon Trail era, 1843 was indeed pivotal in the long historical record of the Pacific Northwest.

Four of the participants (three missionaries and a mountain man) would later come together as board members for Tualatin Academy—Harvey Clark, A. T. Smith, William H. Gray, and Osborne Russell. Each voted for the new provisional government, and each was elected to important leadership roles in the nascent enterprise.

The site of this famous meeting was preserved at Champoeg State Park—known originally as Provisional Government Park—in 1901. During the previous year, the Oregon Historical Society had worked with the last living participant, Francois Xavier Matthieu, to locate the actual gathering spot. A granite obelisk, bearing the names of the 52 pro-American voters, marks the location. Harvey W. Scott, Pacific University's first graduate and the founding president of the Oregon Historical Society, gave the dedication address.

If West Tualatin Plains, little more than an outpost in 1848, was an unlikely place to start such an institution, Harvey Clark was an even less likely candidate to start one. Ironically, his chief qualification for laying the foundation for Pacific University might well have been that he had begun his career as a stonemason. By all accounts, Clark was a good stonemason; an early biographer notes that many of Clark's friends, on learning that he had decided instead to study for the ministry, "were inclined to oppose him, fearing that a good mason would be spoiled in the making of an indifferent minister." A more recent observer, Steven Richardson, commenting on the tendency to mythologize early pioneers, complains of the process by which "a weak-willed Harvey Clark has become someone to name grade schools after in Forest Grove." The point is well taken, though "weak-willed" seems an incongruent epithet for someone who could cross a frontier on horseback to pursue a mission that most of his friends discouraged him from undertaking and that his own church was unwilling to support.

Harvey Clark's cabin in 1890, located near the present day intersection of 15th Avenue and Elm Street in Forest Grove.

Still, Clark was neither a forceful nor a practical man, having little interest in money, no head for business, and a downright aversion to organizational and legal formalities. This latter trait would often land him in hot water with his more fastidious colleagues in Christ. When, as we shall see shortly, they were jointly entertaining the proposition of starting a school, Clark attempted to skirt the issue of establishing a board of trustees, saying, "If the thing does well we will have trustees. It may soon drop, though." His Congregationalist and Presbyterian brethren were aghast at this lackadaisical approach and insisted on establishing a board, a demand to which Clark good-naturedly agreed. Even more appalling was his suggestion that the Bible not be used in the school—this on the grounds that other books were more suitable for children and that much of the Bible was ungrammatical. Such attitudes go far toward explaining why, as Carolyn Buan in her book *A Changing Mission* notes, "The newcomers' [from the Whitman party] initial gratitude to Harvey Clark for taking them in and helping them rebuild their lives was soon replaced by suspicion and resentment."

"Suspicion and resentment," however, must be taken in context, and in this case the context included a plethora of shepherds and a dearth of sheep. The whole of the Oregon Country boasted only a few thousand souls of European ancestry at the time, and at least a tenth of the adult population in the Tualatin Plains settlement consisted of ordained ministers and their wives. Clark, while he often found himself in the thick of old rivalries, new grievances, and petty in-fighting, was not inclined by temperament to join in. For one thing, he lacked the requisite righteousness, being both aware of his own shortcomings and generally tolerant of failings in others. He was, in a word, likeable, and his popularity with the mountain men, their Indian wives, and children of mixed ancestry was itself a cause for resentment. (When, on one occasion, Clark agreed to marry a young couple who had run away from home, he was straightway chastised for pandering to public sentiment.) He was remembered by many of his contemporaries as a kind man who had a ready smile and a joke for everyone. His gifts seem to have been those of the less-than-strong-willed—an understanding of human frailty coupled with an innate generosity, of which we shall see more later.

In many ways, Harvey Clark was a vessel waiting to be filled, and fate, against all the odds, seemed bent on filling it. Among the circumstances that conspired to turn this unexceptional man into "The Father of Forest Grove," none was more fortuitous than his encountering the exceptional woman whom the Oregon State Legislature, in 1987, would officially recognize as "The Mother of Oregon."

"GRANDMA BROWN"

In October of 1847, just a month before the Whitman Massacre, Harvey Clark was sitting in his modest log cabin conversing with one Tabitha Moffatt Brown, who was a house guest of the Clarks at the time. Grandma Brown, as she would come to be known to her younger contemporaries, had been born in 1780 in Brimfield, Massachusetts, the daughter of a physician. She had married Rev. Clark Brown, an Episcopal minister, who died in 1817, leaving his wife to raise their three children. After teaching school in both Maryland and Virginia, she moved to Missouri, from whence her son, Orus, traveled west with the Great Migration Wagon Train to Oregon in 1843. When Orus returned three years later to relocate his family to Oregon, Tabitha Brown decided to join them. She came west along the Oregon Trail in 1846 with her son and his family, her married daughter Pherne, and her 77-year-old brother-in-law, Captain John Brown.

The account of their journey, preserved in Tabitha Brown's now-famous "Brimfield Heroine Letter," has become the stuff of legend—most notably the encounter with "a rascally fellow" who lured them off course with the promise of a "new cut off" that would get them to the settlement in Oregon City long before those who had gone down the Columbia River. The error in judgment was costly, resulting in "sufferings from that time no tongue can tell." The sufferings they endured on the South Road (Applegate Trail) included being bounced along on poor and dangerous roads, losing most of their worldly belongings, barely surviving an early winter storm (the same storm that stranded the famous Donner Party in California), and fighting off starvation when their food supplies ran out. The "shortcut" ended when Tabitha Brown walked into the settlement of Salem, some 50 miles south of Oregon City, on Christmas Day, 1846.

Such anecdotes, however, merely feed the impulse to reduce Tabitha Brown to a caricature, whereas the factual record, including her letters, reveals a bright, resourceful woman with an uncommon share of common sense and a buoyancy of spirit that, a century-and-a-half later, remains contagious. If her pluck has become legendary, it is largely because she was indeed plucky. Before taking up temporary residence in the Clark's cabin, she had, in her own words, "Spent the summer visiting and bathing in the ocean" off Astoria. She was 67 at the time.

On her way back from Astoria to her home in Salem, Tabitha Brown stopped in to see her son Orus, from whom Harvey Clark had acquired land and who introduced her to the Clarks. She recounts the outcome of this introduction in a letter:

> [The Clarks] invited me to spend a few days. Winter set in. They pressed me hard to spend the winter with them. I accepted their invitation. Our intimacy ever since has been more like mother and children than that of strangers. They are about the same age as my own children, and look to me for counsel and advice equally as much.

It is from the same letter that we learn of her conversation with Harvey Clark in October of 1847:

> I said to Mr. Clark one day, "Why has Providence frowned on me and left me poor in this world? Had he blessed me with riches, as he has many others, I know right what I would do." "What would

Top: The printed sermon for the marriage of the Rev. Clark Brown and Miss Tabitha Moffatt on December 1, 1799 in Brimfield, Mass., and a miniature painting of the Rev. Brown.
Below: The only existing portrait of Tabitha Brown taken shortly before her death in 1858.

The Oregon Trail

*T*HE TENSION between Great Britain and the United States over future sovereignty of the Pacific Northwest region caused Americans to push for settlement, reasoning that a strong population base would tip the balance. To many, it was "Manifest Destiny" that the country should spread to the Pacific coast. Before Oregon could even declare itself a Territory of the United States, it needed settlers.

Americans anxious to acquire free land in Oregon began crossing the Plains in large wagon trains in the 1840s, enduring physical hardships and emotional trauma along the 2000-mile route from Independence, Missouri to the Willamette Valley. A family, traveling in a wagon pulled by oxen, could expect a six-month journey, while a man going solo could ride horseback and make it in half the time. Thousands of people used the Oregon Trail for overland migration during the next 20 years.

The Great Migration of 1843—involving nearly 900 men, women, and children—is considered the start of the mass movement to the Oregon Country. Dr. Marcus Whitman, missionary-turned-patriot, led the train from Independence to Oregon. Orus Brown, oldest son of Tabitha and Clark Brown, was among the travelers, venturing alone in order to test the trip's difficulty and benefits before taking his wife and children out into the frontier. Orus Brown searched the Willamette Valley for suitable farmland and eventually decided on West Tualatin Plains as the best location. With help from A.T. Smith, Orus claimed land and constructed a cabin. When he went back to Missouri in 1846 to get his wife and children, Orus allowed Rev. Harvey Clark to acquire his claim.

Many Oregon Trail immigrants were later affiliated with Tualatin Academy and Pacific University. Tabitha Brown's heart-wrenching story of nearly perishing on the South Road, or Applegate Trail, in 1846 is well known. J. Quinn Thornton, another member of that disastrous trip, became a trustee and suggested the name "Forest Grove" for the new town. Harvey W. Scott, Pacific's first graduate, came in 1852 at age 14 with his family, including older sister Abigail. During their difficult trip, Harvey and Abigail lost their mother to cholera.

It was no coincidence that Oregon's provisional government was created in 1843, just as migration to the region increased. In 1846 Great Britain and the United States signed a treaty establishing the northern border of Oregon (now the border between Washington and Canada) at the 49th parallel. Two years later, in 1848, Oregon became a U.S. territory.

Left: Daily journal written by Virgil K. Pringle (Tabitha Brown's son-in-law) while travelling the Oregon Trail in 1846. Virgil and Pherne Brown Pringle settled in Salem.

you do?" "I would establish myself in a comfortable house and receive all the poor children, and be a mother to them." He fixed his keen eyes on me to see if I was candid in what I said. "Yes, I am," said I. "If so, I will try," said he, "to help you."

The "poor children" of whom Tabitha Brown speaks here were mainly those who had lost their parents to hardship or disease along the Oregon Trail. The need for an orphan school, however, would soon become aggravated by yet another historic event. On the morning of January 24, 1848, gold was discovered at Sutter's Mill on the American River in the Sierra foothills of Northern California. By the time the orphan school would become a reality, the Gold Rush would be in full force, luring more than 100,000 fortune-seekers in 1848 alone. In the diaries and minutes of those who chose to stick it out in Forest Grove, the loss of able-bodied men to the gold fields of California would become a recurrent theme, and many of these men who were widowers would leave their children in the care of "Grandma" Brown.

The fruit of Tabitha Brown and Harvey Clark's conversation in 1847 was the "Orphan Asylum," which officially opened in an old log meeting house in the spring of 1848. Neighbors contributed what eating utensils, pans, and dishes they could part with; parents who could afford to pay were charged a dollar a week

for board and tuition; and Tabitha Brown agreed to work as teacher, manager, and housekeeper for the first year without pay. After a trip back to Salem to get her belongings, Grandma Brown returned to the plains in late April and, as she puts it, "Found everything prepared for me to go into the meeting house and cluck up my chickens the next morning."

By the summer of 1848, as James R. Robertson reports in 1905:

the orphan asylum was more than an idea; it was an institution. Something tangible had started. Something had come into being where before there was nothing. It was only a forerunner of what was to follow, but it served its purpose and it had its distinct bearing on subsequent events.

Neither Tabitha Brown nor Harvey Clark could have imagined that subsequent events would include the founding of a university on the site of their orphans' refuge. Nor could they have known that the person who would initiate that unlikely metamorphosis was, at this very moment, waiting for passage to Oregon on a remote island in the South Pacific.

One of the pencil drawings made by Pherne Pringle, Tabitha Brown's married daughter, while crossing the country over the Oregon Trail.

One of the stories responsible for Tabitha Brown's place on the Honor Roll of Oregon Trail characters illustrates her uncanny ability to survive and prosper. In the famous "Brimfield Heroine Letter" she wrote: "For two or three weeks of my journey down the Willamette I had felt something in the end of my glove finger which I supposed to be a button. On examination at my new home in Salem, I found it to be a 6 1/4 cent piece. This was the whole of my cash capital to commence business with in Oregon. With it I purchased three needles. I traded off some of my old clothes to the squaws for buckskins, worked them into gloves for the Oregon ladies and gentlemen, which cleared me upwards of $30 extra of boarding."

The small coin she discovered was a Spanish half-real, like the one pictured here. Called a "picayune" in those days and valued at 1/16 of a dollar, it was the smallest silver coin in circulation. Prior to the Legal Tender Law of 1857, the coins of Spain, Mexico, Columbia, Bolivia, Central America, Peru, Portugal, and Brazil were legal currency in the United States. Most people, especially on the frontier, were very happy to get paid in any kind of silver.

Actual Size

Laying the Foundation: George Atkinson

He [Harvey Clark] last spring commenced what is called an orphan school. It had about forty scholars. … It is a good site and it may grow to some importance. — GEORGE ATKINSON, 1848

REVEREND GEORGE ATKINSON is the only one of Pacific University's three "founders" who is not remembered on the campus with a building in his name—this despite the fact that he conceived the idea of starting an academy that should have a "collegiate department" and that he outlived both Harvey Clark and Tabitha Brown by over 30 years. One reason for this injustice of history, perhaps, was that, for all of his dedication, Atkinson was not a particularly colorful man. To serve as secretary on a college board of trustees for 41 years requires extraordinary qualities, but great imagination is not one of them. Having once put his hand to the plow, however, Atkinson was not a man to look back. He was a by-the-book, nose-to-the-grindstone Congregationalist who had his marching orders to start a college somewhere in Oregon, and nothing was going to stop him.

CATALYST FOR A COLLEGE

News of the Whitman Massacre traveled fast— as fast as anything traveled in the mid-1800s. Out in Honolulu, Oahu (then one of the Sandwich Islands), a 28-year-old missionary named George Atkinson and his wife, Nancy, were waiting for passage to the Oregon Country when news of the event reached them.

Atkinson, a graduate of Dartmouth College and Andover Theological Seminary, had originally intended to serve the Zulu Mission in South Africa, but a delay in his ordination forced him and his new bride to miss the ship bound for Africa, a turn of fate that led them to the Oregon Country. They were sent there by the American Home Missionary Society, which, in 1846, inherited responsibility for the western missions from the American Board of Commissioners for Foreign Missions, the

George Atkinson

group that had sponsored the Whitman party. While visiting New York in May of 1847 to receive instructions about his work, Atkinson was introduced to Dr. Theron Baldwin, secretary of the newly formed American College Society, whose goal it was to establish a Congregational college in every new state. It was from Baldwin that he received his orders to "build an academy that shall grow into a college."

Departing from New York on October 23, 1847, Atkinson and his wife had sailed around the "The Horn" to Honolulu aboard the bark *Samoset*, bound for China, a voyage of 125 days, and would spend three months in Honolulu awaiting another vessel, the *Cowlitz*,

George Atkinson and his family (Forest Grove United Church of Christ Archives)

Below, right: George Atkinson's diploma from Dartmouth College (1843)

and, in July of 1848, only a month after his arrival, arranged a meeting in Clark's log cabin that included, along with Clark, Reverends Henry Spalding, Elkanah Walker, and Lewis Thompson. Besides discussing the prospects for starting an academy, they decided to join forces by forming the Oregon Association of Congregational and New School Presbyterian Ministers, later shortened to the Oregon Association of Churches and Ministers, which held its first annual meeting in Oregon City on September 21 of the same year. Harvey Clark, probably because of his seniority in the region, became the association's president and Atkinson himself became secretary.

It was at this meeting, then, that the newly-formed association determined to start an academy, and to locate it at the site of the Orphan Asylum operated by Rev. Clark and Tabitha Brown. Grandma Brown contributed $500 to the project, and Harvey Clark generously deeded 200 acres of land, a gift that went far toward ensuring the success of the enterprise. Clark and Atkinson drafted a charter for the proposed institution, and on September 26, 1849, the group became legally incorporated, an act that represented the first charter ever granted by the civil government of Oregon.

Both the religious nature and the ultimate purpose of the institution are embedded in

to take them to the Pacific Northwest. Atkinson's Honolulu diary for February 26, 1848, includes this entry:

> Here, we first learned … of the horrible massacre of Dr. Whitman, his wife and nine others, by the Cayuse Indians, among whom he had labored twelve years. The natives were suffering from sickness, and supposed the doctor had been poisoning them to possess their lands. They kill their own doctors on the same suspicion. It will not affect the lower country where we are going.

As we have seen, however, the Whitman Massacre did affect the lower country, which, when Atkinson finally arrived in Oregon City in June of 1848, was teeming with by-now-disgruntled ministers. Determined to start an "academy that shall grow into a college," Atkinson's first task was to create some order out of the sectarian chaos. Hearing of Harvey Clark's venture in West Tualatin Plains, he traveled there by horseback

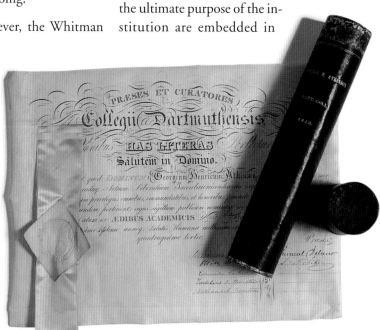

An Act to establish an Academy in Tualatin County.

Sect.1. Be it enacted by the Legislative Assembly of the Territory of Oregon; That there shall be established in Tualatin County, a Seminary of learning for the instruction of persons of both sexes in science and literature, to be called the "Tualatin Academy; and that George H. Atkinson, Harvey Clark, James Moore, Peter H Hatch, Lewis Thompson, William H Gray, Hiram Clark, A. T. Smith and I. L. Thornton, and their successors, are hereby declared to be a body politic and corporate in law by the name and style of "The President and Trustees of the Tualatin Academy."

this original charter, which included a provision for establishing a collegiate department as soon as possible. Robertson notes:

> In this provision for collegiate education [Tualatin Academy] preceded all educational institutions on the Pacific Coast. It may be regarded as one of the acts of splendid audacity with which the student of western history becomes familiar.

"SPLENDID AUDACITY" MEETS STARK REALITY

Securing a charter was one thing; securing a faculty for the academy was another. The first teacher, a young man named D. C. L. Latourette, lasted only six months before he "was unable to resist the allurements of the gold fields of California." The trustees then appointed Whitman-Massacre-refugee Cushing Eells, who lasted only a little longer before leaving in a huff over the school's policy regarding tobacco. Atkinson, with typical lack of affect, reports in his diary:

> Bro. E. has left us unpleasantly situated. He wishes us to prohibit the attendance of all scholars who use tobacco. We prohibited its use in and about the school house. He leaves the school somewhat disaffected with us, we have reason to suppose.

Eells would later manage to overcome his disaffection and rejoin the academy for a longer stay before resigning permanently in 1860 to return to Walla Walla, and found the future

Section 1 of "An Act to Establish an Academy in Tualatin County" chartered Sept. 26, 1849 by the Territorial Legislature "… for the instruction of persons of both sexes in science and literature"

College Hall (now Old College Hall) on its original site in 1892.

Whitman College, whose original tobacco policy is not a matter of public record. By the end of 1851, however, it was clear to the trustees that they would have to send someone east to find a president for the "collegiate department." Atkinson was assigned that task, the outcome of which would prove to be perhaps his most significant contribution to the future of Pacific University.

In the meantime, however, there was the matter of buildings. Originally, classes were held in the log building used by Harvey Clark as the Congregational Church. Plans for a new building began in earnest almost immediately, and the trustees managed to raise the considerable sum of $7,000 to begin construction. The raising of the frame in July 1850 was the occasion for all-out celebration, drawing settlers from near and far to camp out on the campus in tents and join in the festivities. Tabitha Brown, who was in charge of food, wrote in her diary, "Quite a number of the ladies met

and we had a social time." Among the "ladies" was Elkanah Walker's wife, Mary Walker, whose own diary entry on the occasion was less than enthusiastic; she described the new building as "A splendid monument to the folly of somebody," and mused: "Wonder who will live to see it completed and filled with students."

Despite Mary Walker's not unwarranted skepticism, the first classes were held in the new building in October of 1851. The Academy Building, now "Old College Hall," would be moved and renamed more than once, but it remains the oldest building on Pacific University's campus and one of the oldest educational structures in the western United States. Fittingly, its original location is the current site of Marsh Memorial Hall, the most imposing structure on the modern campus, and one whose name serves to introduce us to the man who justifies our referring to Pacific University as "The House that Marsh Built."

The Settlement Gets a Name

*T*HE CITY now called "Forest Grove" lies in an area once known as "West Tualatin Plains." After Tualatin Academy received its charter in 1849, the Board of Trustees decided to create an adjoining town site, selling lots platted on land donated by Rev. Harvey and Emeline Clark. The downtown business district immediately located to the west of campus was part of this new development.

The matter of naming the new town finally came up during two meetings of the Academy's Board of Trustees, held in Oregon City on January 9 and 10, 1851. Original meeting minutes in the Pacific University Archives recorded that on the first day the name "Vernon" was proposed, followed by the question, "Ought [this matter] not to be at once settled?" Apparently the Trustees decided to sleep on it, making a decision the next day. The minutes show the following action taken by the Board:

> Moved by Mr. [George] Atkinson and seconded to call the town, "Vernon." Rejected.

> Moved by Mr. [J. Quinn] Thornton and seconded that the name of the town be "Forest Grove." Passed.

J. Quinn Thornton had arrived in the Willamette Valley in November 1846 following an arduous overland trip on the "damnable Applegate Trail." The Thorntons had already named their land claim "Forest Grove," so it was simply a matter of proposing this favored name for the new town. Thornton had joined the Board of Trustees when mountain man Osborne Russell headed south to the California gold fields.

From the beginning, some recognized the name "Forest Grove" as an oxymoron. Sidney Harper Marsh, for example, insisted on referring to the town simply as "The Grove," perhaps recognizing that a forest can be only so small and a grove only so large before suffering the arboreal equivalent of an identity crisis. In some ways, the contradiction about size implicit in the name "Forest Grove" parallels the conflict about whether the Trustees were starting a college or a university, and foreshadows other recurrent identity issues that would plague the school throughout its history.

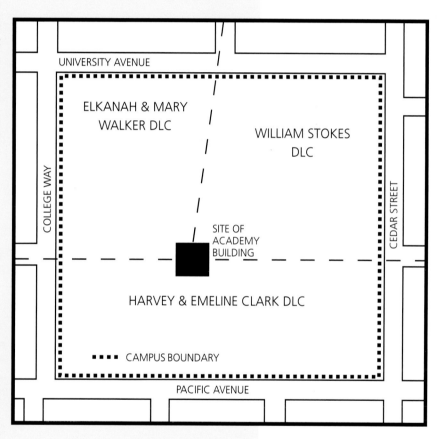

Portions of three Donation Land Claims (DLC) were combined to form the original campus.

Raising the Walls: Sidney Harper Marsh

Forest Grove was in one corner of the settlement, and was almost inaccessible by reason of bad mountain roads. Within a radius of ten miles there were scarcely fifty voters. ... Forest Grove could hardly have been called a village. — SIDNEY HARPER MARSH, 1878

TABITHA BROWN, Harvey Clark, and George Henry Atkinson: that Pacific University came into existence at all was largely due to the efforts of these three pioneers who are formally acknowledged as its "founders." That it came to be what it is, however, is largely due to the vision of one man, Sidney Harper Marsh. Myron Eells, writing of Marsh after his death, said that he was "a man of one idea." That one idea, in Marsh's own words, was "To realize the very special purpose of a liberal education—not merely to develop the powers needed to make a living, but all the powers, physical, intellectual and spiritual, preparing the man to do his part of God's work in the world." To a remarkable degree, Marsh's idea—modified by the exigencies of place, people, and economic pressures—is embodied in the present-day institution that we know as Pacific University.

HEEDING THE CALL

New York City, November, 1852: huge crowds daily throng the streets to watch a colossal edifice of glass and iron—arched, columned, turreted, and topped with the largest dome America has ever seen—springing up as if by magic not far from the future site of the New York Public Library. The entire city is in the throes of preparing for a great international event, the World's Fair of 1853. Within earshot of the construction, in Union Theological Seminary at University Place, a 27-year-old seminarian named Sidney Harper Marsh has received an invitation to meet with George Atkinson of Forest Grove, Oregon, to discuss an educational venture in the wilds of the Pacific Northwest.

The young man whom George Atkinson was about to interview was no stranger to adversity. A Southerner by birth—he had been born at Hampden-Sidney College, Virginia in

Sidney Harper Marsh, who came from a long line of prominent educators, was without doubt the guiding force behind Pacific University's early character and direction. A man of great intelligence and firm principles, he bore the burdens of president, teacher, fund-raiser, and father with unflinching dedication and unfailing good humor. Even in this typically somber photo, one can detect in Marsh's face the hint of a suppressed and slightly sardonic smile.

James Marsh, Father of Pacific's First President

JAMES MARSH, father of Sidney Harper Marsh and a key figure in American Transcendentalism, was born on July 19, 1794 in Hartford, Vermont. James was intended to follow in his father's footsteps and manage the large family farm, while his brother, Roswell, had been elected to go to Dartmouth. But Roswell balked at the indignity of carrying a leg of mutton off to college in partial payment of his board and ran away from home, leaving the way to Dartmouth open for James.

James Marsh

It was at Dartmouth, which in 1813 was still awash in the eddies of the Second Great Awakening, that Marsh converted to Congregationalism. He began his studies for the ministry at Andover Theological Seminary in 1817 and, after returning to Dartmouth for two years as a tutor, graduated from Andover in 1822. In the following year, he went to Hampton-Sidney, Virginia to teach oriental languages, and in 1824 married Lucia Wheelock, granddaughter of Eleazer Wheelock, the founder of Dartmouth College, and a niece of John Wheelock, a former president of Dartmouth. Their only child, Sidney Harper Marsh, was born on August 29, 1825. A mere three years later, Lucia Wheelock Marsh died of tuberculosis, leaving James a widower until 1830, when he married Lucia's sister, Laura Wheelock. Laura became the mother of Joseph Walker Marsh before she too succumbed to tuberculosis in 1838. Strictly speaking, then, Sidney Harper Marsh and Joseph Walker Marsh, pivotal players in Pacific University's early days, were both half-brothers (three-quarter brothers?) and cousins.

Chroniclers of Pacific's early years routinely note that James Marsh served as president of the University of Vermont (1826–1833). None of them seems aware, however, that he was also a major influence on the thinking of such giants in American literature as Ralph Waldo Emerson and Henry David Thoreau. In 1829 Marsh edited Samuel Taylor Coleridge's *Aids to Reflection*, thus becoming the link between English Romanticism and what would become American Transcendentalism. Marsh's introduction to the book fired Emerson's imagination and became a touchstone of his thought. Robert Richardson in his biography *Emerson, The Mind on Fire*, notes of Marsh's introduction: "Here was a sober, modern, defensible, intellectually rigorous account of the nature of the power that resides in each individual soul. Marsh's formulation became over the next few years a conviction Emerson would hold for the rest of his life."

(For more on James Marsh's influence on Transcendentalism, see Peter Carafiol's *Transcendent Reason: James Marsh and the Forms of Romantic Thought*.)

1825—and a New Englander by education, Sidney Marsh had lost his mother when he was three, then his stepmother (his mother's sister) shortly after turning 13, and finally his father at the age of 17, when the elder Marsh was president of the University of Vermont and Sidney was already a student there. The Reverend James Marsh had been only 48 when he died of lung disease. He had passed on to his son not only an abiding dedication to the ideals of liberal education, but also a lifelong pulmonary condition, which, at the time of Atkinson's invitation, was weighing heavily on young Sidney's mind.

The two men met in Brooklyn in that November of 1852, and we know little of what transpired at the meeting. Was Atkinson, a graduate of Dartmouth College, aware that he was interviewing the great-grandson of Dartmouth's founder and first president, Eleazer Wheelock? What we do know, however, is that a letter from Atkinson formally offering a position was waiting for the young Marsh when he arrived back at Union Theological Seminary. He responded immediately:

My lungs are proving themselves too sensitive for this climate, and for a few days especially I have been thinking that mi-

gration to Florida or some warmer climate would be better than remaining here. Under such circumstances ... your letter seemed almost Providential, and I feel like assenting at once to what I understand you to propose.

Never mind that neither man could have fully understood what was being proposed (Marsh was formally hired as an instructor for an academy; within a year he would be appointed first president of a new college). Never mind that Oregon's climate was a far cry from Florida's. The voice of Providence had spoken, and Sidney Marsh had heard the call.

With characteristic enthusiasm and industry, Marsh spent the following winter and spring rounding up a library of over 1,000 books for the prospective college. He even managed to attract the notice of the *New York Times*, which, mistakenly identifying him as the nephew (actually cousin) of the U.S. Ambassador to Constantinople, commended his efforts and wished the new enterprise well.

On May 1, 1853, Sidney Marsh was ordained in the Church of the Pilgrims in Brooklyn, New York. He would set out by sea on his own pilgrimage to the West a month later, shortly after the grand opening of the World's

Academy Hall, which can be distinguished from Old College Hall by its four chimneys, was built in 1864 and destroyed by fire in 1910. This "twin" building to Old College Hall stood on the site of the Harvey W. Scott Memorial Library.

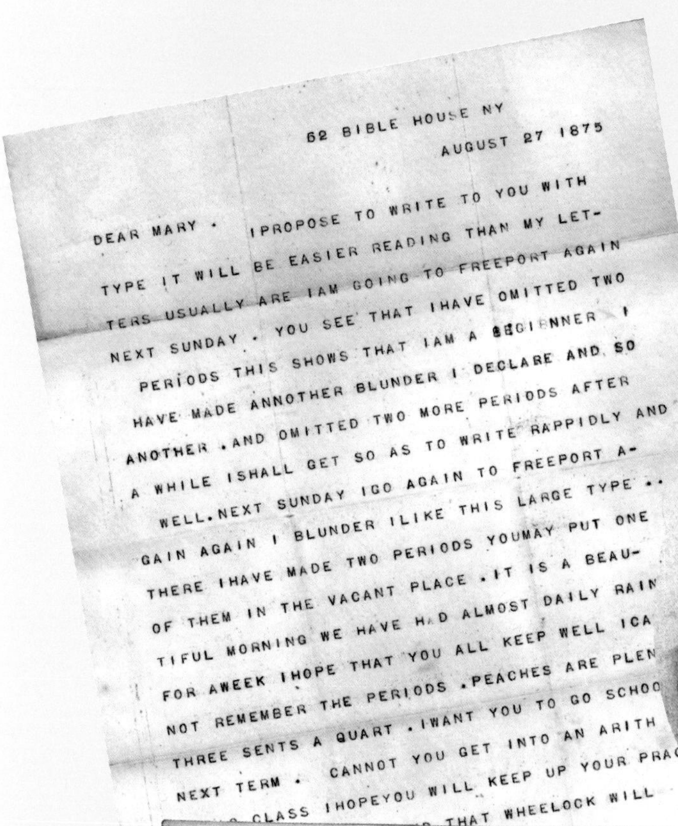

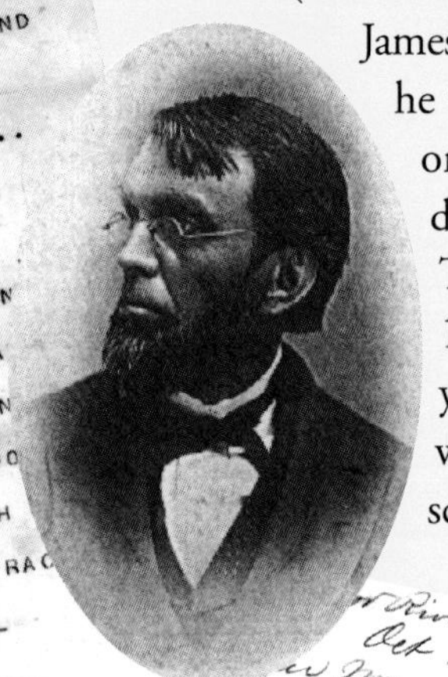

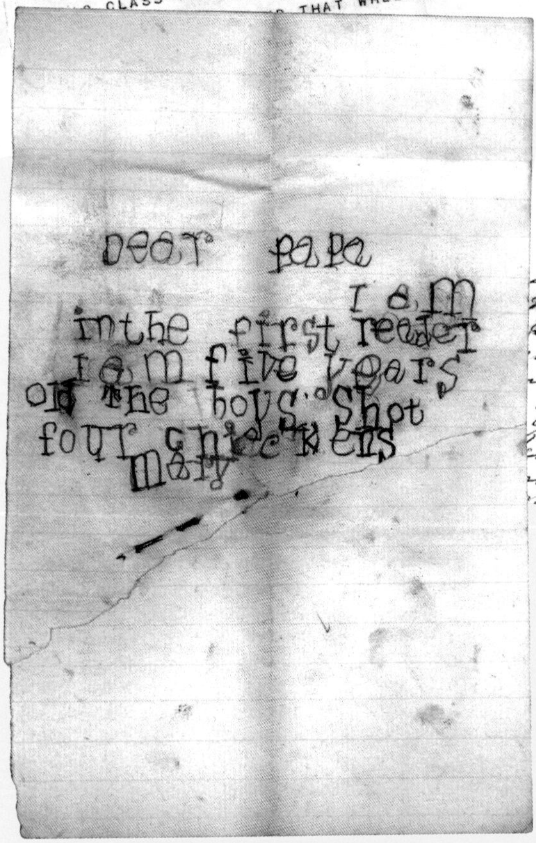

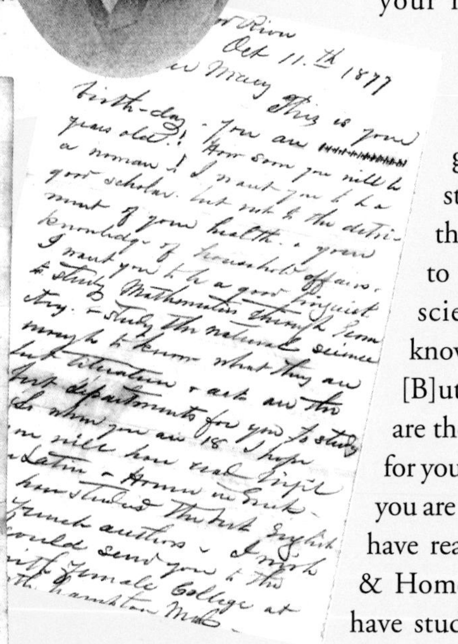

SIDNEY HARPER MARSH'S human side emerges in the correspondence with his family, especially his children. Below, left, his daughter Mary displays her penmanship for her father at age five; in a letter to Mary when she is 10, Marsh has some fun with a new-fangled machine called a "typewriter" (the "Wheelock" referred to is Marsh's son, James Wheelock Marsh); two years later, he writes to Mary from Hood River on the occasion of her 13th birthday. The text reads: "Dear Mary This is your birth-day. You are 1+1+1+1+1+1+1+1+1+1+1+1+1 years old! How soon you will be a woman! I want you to be a good scholar, but not to the detriment of your health and your knowledge of household affairs. I want you to be a good linguist, to study Mathematics through Geometry, to study the natural sciences enough to know what they are[.] [B]ut literature & arts are the first department for you to study. So when you are 18 I hope you will have read Virgil in Latin & Homer in Greek, and have studied the best English and French authors. I wish I could send you to the Smith Female College at Northhampton, Mass." Marsh died two years after this letter was written, and his daughter Mary died a year after that. She was 16.

62 BIBLE HOUSE NY
AUGUST 27 1875

DEAR MARY . IPROPOSE TO WRITE TO YOU WITH
TYPE IT WILL BE EASIER READING THAN MY LET-
TERS USUALLY ARE IAM GOING TO FREEPORT AGAIN
NEXT SUNDAY . YOU SEE THAT IHAVE OMITTED TWO
PERIODS THIS SHOWS THAT IAM A BEGINNER I
HAVE MADE ANNOTHER BLUNDER I DECLARE AND SO
ANOTHER .AND OMITTED TWO MORE PERIODS AFTER
A WHILE ISHALL GET SO AS TO WRITE RAPPIDLY AND
WELL.NEXT SUNDAY IGO AGAIN TO FREEPORT A-
GAIN AGAIN I BLUNDER ILIKE THIS LARGE TYPE ..
THERE IHAVE MADE TWO PERIODS YOUMAY PUT ONE
OF THEM IN THE VACANT PLACE .IT IS A BEAU-
TIFUL MORNING WE HAVE HAD ALMOST DAILY RAIN
FOR AWEEK IHOPE THAT YOU ALL KEEP WELL ICA
NOT REMEMBER THE PERIODS .PEACHES ARE PLEN
THREE SENTS A QUART .IWANT YOU TO GO SCHOO
NEXT TERM . CANNOT YOU GET INTO AN ARITH
CLASS IHOPEYOU WILL KEEP UP YOUR PRAC
THAT WHEELOCK WILL

Dear papa
I am
in the first reader
I am five years
old The boys shot
four chickens
mary

Oct 11th 1877
Mary This is your
birth-day. You are
years old! How soon you will be
a woman! I want you to be a
good scholar but not to the detriment of your health & your
knowledge of household affairs.
I want you to be a good linguist
to study Mathematics through Geometry, to study the natural science
enough to know what they are
but literature & arts are the
first departments for you to study
So when you are 18 I hope
you will have read Virgil
Latin & Homer in Greek
have studied the best English
French authors. I wish
could send you to the
Smith Female College at
Northhampton Mass.

Fair. He could hardly have missed it: cannons roared, bells peeled, an inaugural chorus sang, and President Franklin Pierce himself, on his steed Black Warrior, led the procession past the exhibitions of intricate machinery, wood carvings, musical instruments, paintings by European masters, and the grand centerpiece—a life-size marble statue of Christopher Columbus, his left hand resting on a globe of the world, and his right hand pointing to a remote spot on that globe—probably not Forest Grove.

THE "AMERICAN SCHOLAR" GOES WEST

To-day, Pacific University … assumes a position from which there is no honorable retreat. After five years of preparation, of painful and strenuous effort, this institution takes a step in advance; the idea of education has taken a higher form of development; the Academy has become the College.

Thus begins the inaugural address of Pacific University's first president, Sidney Marsh, whose "idea of education" at the age of 28 would guide the new college for the next quarter of a century. To understand that idea, and how it must have struck many of those who listened to these words, we need to place it in the context of the New England soil from which it sprang.

In 1853, the year that Sidney Marsh arrived in Forest Grove, Ralph Waldo Emerson was at the height of his career as an essayist and lecturer, and Henry David Thoreau had just finished reading Darwin's recently published *Voyage of the Beagle,* and was busy writing the fourth draft of *Walden.* It is unlikely that Marsh had heard of Thoreau, who, even after *Walden* was published, remained relatively obscure. But he would certainly have known of Emerson and, like many another young man of the time, had probably read and been fired up by the great man's essays, including the famous "The American Scholar." Originally delivered as a Phi Beta Kappa address at Harvard in 1837, "The American Scholar" is a paean to the practical adequacy of the individual, the imperative of self-reliance, and the superiority of the whole person to the specialist: "If the single man plant himself indomitably on his instincts, and there abide, the huge world will come round to him." Ironically, many of Emerson's central ideas here derived from his reading of an introduction to Coleridge's *Aids to Reflection* that had been written in 1829 by James Marsh, Sidney Marsh's father. Consequently, the younger Marsh, whether or not he had read Emerson, had probably been exposed to these transcendentalist notions from his earliest years.

Speculation aside, the Emersonian spirit permeates Marsh's inaugural address as Presi-

Woodcut of the Pacific University campus (ca. 1870) looking west and showing (left to right) Forest Grove Congregational Church, College Hall, Marsh House (now Walker Hall), and Academy Hall.

Moving Left and Moving West: Congregationalism in the 19th Century

Forest Grove Congregational Church (ca. 1870) stands on the site of the current Forest Grove United Church of Christ (Congregational), at the intersection of 21st Avenue and College Way.

$\mathcal{T}$HE CONGREGATIONAL CHURCH'S origins lay with those Puritans who crossed the ocean in the seventeenth century to create what their leader, John Winthrop, called a "city upon a hill." In the seventeenth century, Puritans achieved a powerful synthesis of religion and government, one that was grounded in human weakness and depravity, and an inability to influence God's decision in the great drama of the soul's eternal destiny. Dealing with a disagreeable humanity, these New Englanders stressed social cohesion above individual liberty, and devised community and familial controls to ensure that the former was not destroyed by the latter. By the nineteenth century, this synthesis faced a number of threats.

One came from within. By 1805, the "Unitarian" wing of the church had captured Harvard Divinity School for those who rejected Divine predestination and placed their faith in human reason and will. This, in turn, led Rev. Jedediah Morse, (father of inventor Samuel Morse) to gather a contingent of like-minded conservatives, whom he advised to "guard against the insidious encroachment of innovation," and establish Andover Theological Seminary, a bastion of Congregationalist orthodoxy from which George Atkinson and others of Pacific University's early leaders were to come.

Thomas Jefferson's election as President provided another challenge to the Puritan synthesis. Jefferson carried Enlightenment principles to their logical conclusion and celebrated the ability of common men to command their own destinies. For orthodox Congregationalists, this threatened to destroy community and open the floodgates of licentious behavior. Economic change reinforced political change as urbanization led to the breakdown of village controls on personal behavior. In this new context, these latter-day Puritans concluded that preserving their moral mission would require Morse's dreaded "innovation." They responded with a burst of energy that would have an important impact on the Northwest and, ultimately, Pacific University.

Out of these conflicting forces a more liberal doctrine emerged, one that stressed human choice over the drama of salvation and even over the very existence of sin itself. Whereas Puritans had believed that sin and corruption were inherent in human life and needed to be controlled, the more liberal Congregationalists of the second quarter of the nineteenth century told their converts that their own salvation was not enough; converts now had to work to eradicate sin from American society. More consistent with the Jeffersonian emphasis on freedom of choice, this revision in the New England way would have a powerful impact on American culture; it would even make inroads at Andover Seminary. In the wake of countless revivals, societies sprang up that were dedicated to temperance, the eradication of prostitution, and the abolition of slavery. One of the leading revivalists, Charles Finney, would help turn the newly formed Oberlin College, alma mater of Pacific founder, Harvey Clark, into a hotbed of antislavery sentiment.

Moreover, Finney and other preachers fostered a vision of female moral superiority, urging women to become active in moral reform. One of these women, Catharine Beecher, sister of Harriet Beecher Stowe, argued that the best way to instill morality in the wide-open American environment, especially in the West, was to educate women as mothers and teachers. As she put it: "The proper education of a man decides the welfare of an individual; but educate a woman, and the interests of a whole family are secured." In keeping with these principles, Oberlin College would break with the practices of American men's colleges and admit female students—a practice that was carried over by the founders of Pacific University.

This highly-charged reform Protestantism spread with the Congregationalist and Presbyterian churches. Under the so-called "Plan of Union" (1801), adherents of the two churches united in their efforts to bring religion and civilization to the West, and they established an organizational infrastructure that included the American Board of Commissioners for Foreign Missions (1810), the American Bible Society (1816), and the American Tract Society (1825). A roadblock to their efforts appeared when Presbyterian conservatives—those who had recommitted themselves to predestinarian theology as it was taught at Princeton Theological Seminary—seized control of the General Assembly and dissolved the Plan of Union. However, the New England reformers of both churches continued to cooperate, jointly establishing Union Theological Seminary in New York City, from whence Pacific's first president would come.

Many Congregationalists, no matter how liberal or orthodox their theology was, considered clerical and missionary activity in the West a patriotic as well as a religious duty. For some—like Samuel F. B. Morse, the son of the founder of Andover Seminary—the West was the stage on which the religious wars of the sixteenth and seventeenth century would be refought, and a religiously-inspired democracy was best able to win the victory. Morse considered "the Bible, the Tract, the Infant school, the Sunday school, the common school for all classes, the college and university" as the "weapons of Protestantism, weapons unknown to Popery." In 1835 he called on right thinkers to make "an immediate, a vigorous, a united, a persevering effort to spread religious and intellectual cultivation through every part of the country." And he argued that the Northwest in particular would be fertile soil, since the Indians in the area had "noble traits of mind." To ensure a bountiful harvest, Morse argued that the church had to take the lead in stopping the "extermination process," and become involved in raising "the oppressed Indian to the comforts and happiness of civilized life."

Thus, by the time the Whitmans and the Spaldings traversed the continent to establish their missions, Congregationalists and liberal Presbyterians had wedded an assertive and benevolent Protestantism to democratic purpose. Despite the tragedy of the Whitman Massacre, these religious reformers would continue their efforts to teach individuals to choose salvation and civilization. At Pacific, their legacy would be felt for decades, in strictures against alcohol and tobacco, in the advocacy of female education, in the continuing emphasis on service, especially in the preparation of students for missionary work, and in the tragic, but well-intentioned attempt of the Indian school to turn young Native Americans into individuals bereft of their cultural inheritance.

*Top: Elisee Meresse (right), instructor in French,
with his Tualatin Academy class (ca. 1900)
on the steps of Marsh Hall.
Above: Pacific University tent at Chautauqua in 1898
Right: Tualatin Academy graduating class in 1888*

Walker Hall: (left) Sidney Harper Marsh died in this small frame house, which was built in 1859 on College Way across from the campus. The house was remodeled in 1946 and named for Charles L. Walker of Hillsboro, a 1906 graduate who left his estate to the university. It currently houses philosophy faculty offices and two classrooms.

Knight Hall: (right) Shortly after Sidney Marsh's death in 1879, his wife and five children moved into the large Victorian house next door—under construction as the new family home when Marsh died—and lived there for many years. Purchased for the university years later, this house is now known as Knight Hall. According to a long-standing campus myth, the house is haunted by a female spirit named "Vera"; every Halloween, radio and TV stations contact the university to inquire about Vera and her activities.

Eliza Haskell Marsh (center), Sidney Marsh's wife

dent of Pacific University in 1854. He speaks of "a wisdom that we all have, that we cannot understand":

> … living ideas, those strong convictions of what is best, derived from former generations, from the race to which we belong … ideas and convictions, whether imbibed with our mothers' milk or developed by external influences, that we feel to be obligatory upon us … that we should be unnatural not to acknowledge.

Marsh's defense of learning—for that is what his inaugural address amounts to—is that "an undeniable impulse has driven man to seek it, and there is an innate respect for it":

> These studies are indeed valuable for other ends, but chiefly because they tend to satisfy the craving thirst for knowledge, which our souls demand, not for their pleasure, or temporary happiness, but for their permanent well-being.

All of this, with the possible exception of the respectful nod to "former generations," echoes the basic tenets of American Transcendentalism, of which Emerson, "The Sage of Concord," was the chief spokesman.

But this was not Concord, and one wonders how these lofty phrases, these paeans to "knowledge as its own reward" must have fallen on the ears of the necessarily practical-minded folk of Forest Grove. Myron Eells, writing in 1881, sums it up: "The educational atmosphere was not in sympathy with a thorough education … the great majority of the people had come from the frontiers and mines, people who were good-hearted and kind, but whose early training and want of advantages had been such that they could not appreciate its benefits." Marsh himself, recalling his inauguration a quarter of a century later, admits that he must have "seemed as one that theorized."

The simple fact is that Sidney Marsh was more than George Atkinson, or anyone else in Forest Grove, had bargained for. Atkinson had foreseen a small college, and a Congregationalist one at that; Marsh, ever the visionary, insisted on calling the new institution a "university," and would spend a good part of his tenure fighting tooth and nail to avoid Congregationalist control. To many of the Forest Grove Congregationalists, the chief enemy was religious in nature—rival denominations, Roman Catholics, and, above all, the Jesuits; to Marsh it was decidedly secular—the rising spectre of scientific materialism that would receive such a boost from the publication of Darwin's *The Origin of Species* in 1859, just five years after Marsh's inauguration. Marsh was not anti-science, but as the son of a beloved father who had served for many years

The Early Connection with Japan

Kin Saito

I N 1876 PACIFIC BECAME one of the first colleges in the United States to grant degrees to students from Japan. During the mid-nineteenth century, the Japanese emperor Mutsuhito came to power, ending the military rule enjoyed by the Shoguns for about 700 years. The restored emperor, known by his reign name "Meiji," urged his people to seek knowledge in all parts of the world to help make Japan strong.

By 1870 Pacific University had enrolled one Japanese student—Hatsutara Tamura—and was actively recruiting others. Three graduates—Hatsutara Tamura, Agero Nosei, and Kin Saito—completed their residency in "The Grove" in 1876 but maintained contact with their primary mentor, President Sidney Harper Marsh, until his death three years later. The following excerpts from their letters to Marsh bear witness to the difficulties they encountered upon leaving Pacific, and to the affection they bore their Alma Mater and its first president.

HATSUTARA TAMURA TO PRESIDENT MARSH

[San Francisco, June 15, 1876]

Sir.… Just before our parting, I wanted to give fully my thanks to you & Mrs. Marsh, but when I shook hands with you, I felt so badly that I could hardly speak a word to you, which no doubt you noticed there. I believe, my <u>silent</u> tears which filled my eyes expressed the feelings within my heart more <u>loudly</u> & <u>forcibly</u> than any audible language would.

[Ellicott City, MD, Sept. 28, 1876]

I have so many things to write that I am almost at a loss as to what to select to begin with. At first I intended to stop in California & attend the State University, but this year the institution made a new regulation requiring new students to pay the tuition of $75.00 for the first year. This change in the in-

Hatsutara Tamura

stitution together with the Grand Fair at Philadelphia induced me to change my mind & go East. Accordingly I left San Francisco on the 28th of July & after a tiresome journey of seven days & nights arrived in Phil. …

Agero Nosei

From Phil. I went to New York & had the pleasures of visiting & seeing different parts of the city. I called on all of your friends whose names you have written in my memorandum. …While I was in New York I became acquainted with the Head Master of an institution called St. Clement's Hall. He offered me a position in his school. Though the school is not so high as I desire it to be, yet being as yet a stranger here I do not expect to get any better place than this & so accepted the position. …

I suppose your school has already been opened & prospering as ever. … I wish you to tell Mary [Marsh's daughter] that I passed through Cleveland, O. within a short distance from the place where Martha [Mary's cousin] lives.

I expect that I will be kept busy hereafter & unable to write as often as I desire to do.…

Your Friend

AGERO NOSEI TO PRESIDENT MARSH

[San Francisco, June 27, 1876]

Dear Sir

I should have written to you soon after our arrival, but my place being unsettled, I delayed it ever so long. Since I left the Grove, I have been wandering around without doing anything. … I could not find any employment. If I stay in this city and get some work, and attend the university at the same time, I might accomplish what I want, but if I do so, it will spend time, and cost. … City living costs so much. I have already spent about $100 since I left the Grove. I think it is better to go home once, and get some position there, and after storing some money, I will come back to this country. I can make money easier in Japan than in this country. I think I can make $100 per month without much difficulty. So now I decided to go home on the next steamer which will leave this city on the 1st of July. …

All three of Pacific's first Japanese graduates eventually returned to Japan and followed careers in education.

Thomas Condon
Pioneer Geologist

Missionary-turned-geologist Rev. Thomas Condon served the University as a Trustee (see letter) and professor from 1873 to 1876, before joining the faculty of the new State University in Eugene. His discovery of the John Day Fossil Beds, and other pioneering work in geology, established him as a leading figure in Oregon's emerging scientific community.

The Dalles Jan 14 1873

Rev Dr Atkinson

Your note of the 8th inst, informing me of my election to the board of trustees of Tual'ite and Pac' University was duly received.

I thank the board for their confidence and yourself especially for what I feel to be your share of it.

I have too many hopes for Oregon's future clustering around the growth of that institution to permit me to decline any part of the work of sustaining it which its friends assign me, and therefore accept the trust you tender

Truly Yours

Thomas Condon

Members of the Marsh family under the "Bee Tree" (said to be Tabitha Brown's source for honey) in 1910. The oak stood between Marsh and Carnegie Halls and was felled in the late 1940s for safety reasons.

as professor of moral and intellectual philosophy, he deplored the idea of scientists assuming the mantle of moral authority.

Mainly, both by temperament and training, Marsh detested narrow thinking of all kinds, and one of his greatest challenges as president would be learning to understand provincialism at least to the point of being able to deal with it effectively. That he never entirely succeeded in this is evident from a speech that he gave to the Board of Trustees of Pacific University in 1878, the year before his death and 25 years after his inaugural address.

Placed side by side, these two documents speak tomes about the first quarter-century of Pacific University. In Marsh's later address, the original vision remains intact, but the idealism of youth has been tempered at the forge of administrative duties. Marsh speaks of how "Spirits and energy were frittered away by unnecessary cares and anxieties which yet I could not avoid," and calls it "the greatest event of my life" that, "At last, after 25 years … the community among whom I had lived so long had come to see what I was 'driving at' and what was meant by a College."

But he spends the greater portion of his 1878 address discussing the two matters that had plagued him from the start and that he would most liked to have rid himself entirely: the financial security and the "denominational relations" of the institution. As we shall see, the two issues were not unrelated.

"MISERABLE BUSINESS"

From the beginning, Pacific University had been heavily dependent on Congregationalist support, most notably on the American College Society, for the salaries of the president and the instructors—$600 in 1853 and $1,200 for the following five years. By 1858, the same year that founders Tabitha Brown and Harvey Clark died, it had become clear that a more secure endowment was needed, and R. T. Baldwin, secretary of the College Society, sent President Marsh a free pass to New York on what would be the first of four protracted trips east to solicit funds. This was one of the duties of a president that Sidney Marsh did not "fully understand," and that he never fully resigned himself to.

That he was good at it, however, is clear from the record. On his first trip east, which kept him away from the college for almost three years, Marsh managed to raise $22,000 in subscriptions and $1,200 in books. He also met and wed Eliza Haskell, by whom he would have eight children, three of whom died before their father.

Five years later we find Marsh back in the East again for a full year, this time returning with over $25,000 for the general endowment. Marsh hated the work. Writing home to his wife during this trip, he notes: "I can get ten thousand here without much doubt. But this is miserable business. I despise the reputation that I am getting by it." Or again:

> Have got one subscripton of one hundred dollars, and two of fifty. Notwithstanding, am miserable. One cannot butt his head against a stone wall twenty times a day without getting a headache, even though once in a while he knocks down a few stones. I have $23,500 done—want to get $1,500 more. So long as I make progress I shall stick to it.

"So long as I make progress I shall stick to it"—this might well have been Sidney Marsh's epitaph. The progress that he made during his tenure as president of Pacific University is summarized in a small memorial pamphlet published on the occasion of his death in 1879:

> President Marsh found Pacific University as a small academy, with scholars not much if any further advanced than those in common school ought to be; with a single building, nothing of a library … and not a dollar of endowment except that the interest on ten thousand dollars had been pledged by the College Society, through the efforts of Dr. Atkinson. He left it with two buildings, and funds partially pledged for a third, with about

Top: The University "Golden Jubilee" celebration on June 16, 1898
Bottom: University Falls, located in the Coast Range, is supposedly named for Pacific University. According to some accounts, a faculty member and his students visited the falls in the 1890s and named the landmark.

five thousand volumes and eight hundred pamplets in the library … while the institution was worth $91,086.38, and forty-nine persons had graduated from the University.

LEGACY OF A LEADER

Despite Sidney Marsh's arduous work and impressive successes on behalf of the college, he was not universally popular as a president. When, at the age of 53, he finally lost his long battle with tuberculosis on February 2, 1879, the memorial reviews from the faculty were mixed. "Not everyone was able to understand his objects," one mourner observed, "nor did they always commend themselves when understood." And another: "He had the nerve to do right as he saw the right, and the man who does so will have enemies." Still a third put his finger on what was unquestionably the sore spot of Marsh's administration: "Dr. Marsh was a Congregationalist, and while he subscribed to the Congregational faith, yet he ever strove to make Pacific University an unsectarian, Christian school."

These last, at the time of Marsh's death, were fighting words to some in the audience who counted themselves as Marsh's enemies, at least on the sectarian issue. While President Marsh held the administrative reins, few of them had entertained any serious hope of overriding his commitment to the ideal of a liberal arts university free from the narrow bounds of sectarianism. He had never pulled any punches on that matter, as this passage from one of his letters to the Board illustrates:

I do not expect support from a good many Congregationalist ministers, and repudiate the interference of such in what is not their affair, when they talk and act as if they had some authority above the constituted authority of the Board of Trustees. We want friends, but intelligent friends if possible. I would welcome the co-operation of any one, so he did not assume to dictate. But to Roman Catholics and Congregationalists alike I say the same thing. I invite their inspection. If the Roman Catholic likes it, I am glad of it, and am sorry if either he or the Congregationalist does not, and in the case of the latter, cannot help being disappointed and grieved. My position repels no one.

But, of course, such a position had repelled many. And when Sidney Marsh died in 1879, many of those who favored a strong Congregationalist bent to the college emerged from the proverbial woodwork. The final irony of Marsh's presidency was that for all of the original resistance to calling the prospective institution a "university," the more dubious word in the school's name at the time of his death might well have been "Pacific."

Left to right: John Bailey, a trustee of Pacific, Clara White Cooley, director of conservatory, Mrs. John Bailey, and Robert S. McClelland, student and nephew of Rev. Thomas McClelland, Pacific's president from 1891 to 1900

Harvey W. Scott: Pacific's First Graduate

PACIFIC University was singularly fortunate in having Harvey Whitefield Scott as its first graduate in 1863. Scott's subsequent career at the *Portland Oregonian* newspaper—he was editor there for 40 years—influenced attitudes and shaped the development of Oregon and the Pacific Northwest. His professional stature gave the university prestige and notoriety among Oregon colleges.

Scott's life reads like a dime-store novel about the self-made man. He travelled to the Northwest when he was only 14 years old, moving overland on the Oregon Trail with his family. Along the way, young Harvey lost his mother and a younger brother. Shortly after arriving on the frontier, he enrolled in Pacific University and took classes between odd jobs, eventually graduating as a class of one (earning the first baccalaureate degree awarded in the entire region). During his time on campus, Scott gained the respect of Sidney Harper Marsh and the trustees, who went so far as to appoint him principal of Tualatin Academy for a short time before he had finished his full course.

As he witnessed the evolution of Portland into a small metropolitan area with industrial and commercial strength, Scott led the move to host the Lewis and Clark Centennial Exposition in 1905, serving as president of the Exposition board in 1903–04. Always interested in Oregon history and cultural develop-ment, he was elected to serve as founding president of the Oregon Historical Society from 1898–1901. Harvey Scott has also been remembered as the younger brother of Abigail Scott Duniway, Oregon's leader in the fight for women's rights. Their differing opinions and journalistic feuds became one of the most well-known sibling rivalries in the nation.

Thirty-eight years after graduation, Scott returned as a member of Pacific University's Board of Trustees in 1901. Only four years later, in 1905, he assumed the position of board president and remained in this role until his death in 1910.

Scott's legacy lives on in the form of the Harvey W. Scott Memorial Library, constructed in 1967. A large portion of the funding for this capital project came from the bequest made by his deceased daughter, Judith Scott Walter (she was also responsible for Walter Hall, a women's residence hall).

Throughout the course of his long life, Scott was a persistent reader and collector of books. His extensive personal library was donated to Pacific University in 1943 and is now part of the Harvey W. Scott Memorial Library collection.

Scott's death in August, 1910, elicited an outpouring of recognition and praise from the nation's major newspapers, of which the excerpts at right are a few examples.

Mr. Scott was an editor who put his personality into the journal which he directed and made it a force to be reckoned with in Oregon life. He was a builder and a counsellor whose services will be greatly missed.

—NEW YORK TRIBUNE

He left a splendid legacy of ideals to the profession of journalism. He made the *Portland Oregonian* one of the great newspapers of the nation.

—NEW YORK EDITOR AND PUBLISHER

He was one of the big men of the West. The esteem in which he was held, the character of the paper he built up, amply testify to the fact that he fully measured up to the occasion.

—BALTIMORE NEWS

Harvey W. Scott was one of America's great editors and one of its leading citizens. By sheer force of his personality and his powerful pen he made himself the leading figure of the Pacific Coast.

—PROVIDENCE JOURNAL

Raising the Roof: Sectarian or Non-sectarian?

The controversy between the churches and the Institution has an ugly look & I wish some means might be devised to do away with it entirely. — THOMAS McCLELLAND, 1891

EXCEPT FOR THE PRACTICAL MATTER of adequate funding to keep the enterprise afloat, the single most important issue that President Marsh and his immediate successors had to deal with was the question of whether the college would fall under Congregationalist control or remain non-sectarian. Until that issue was settled, the future direction—indeed, the very nature—of the college would remain in question.

A HARD ACT TO FOLLOW: PRESIDENT HERRICK

James Rood Robertson, principal of Tualatin Academy from 1890–93 and professor of history at the university from 1893–1906, noted with not-too-distant hindsight in 1905, that "The selection of a successor to President Marsh was not an easy matter and considerable time elapsed before the choice was finally made." And considerable in-fighting. Significantly, while the trustees were busy lobbying for various candidates sympathetic to their individual views, the role of acting president fell to Marsh's half-brother, Joseph Marsh, who, as Robertson notes, "was familiar with the policies of his brother."

Joseph Walker Marsh, 10 years younger than his brother and a 12-year veteran faculty member in classical languages at the time of Marsh's death, was not only familiar with his brother's "policies," but shared his views. Moreover, his assuming the role of acting president at this crucial juncture in the college's history was somewhat unusual. That function, during the several periods when Sidney Marsh had been off in the East trying to drum up funds, had consistently fallen to Rev. Horace Lyman,

who had seniority over Joseph Marsh, having served as chair of mathematics since 1857. Lyman was, by all reports, an excellent, even an inspiring, teacher; but he was also a scientist. Science, as we have noted, was not a field of endeavor dear to the heart of Sidney Harper Marsh; the scientific equipment available to students during his tenure consisted of a spyglass for looking at the stars and a galvanic battery that Professor Lyman owned and used mainly as a curative for rheumatism.

In addition, Lyman was a close personal friend of George Atkinson, having, like Atkinson, attended Andover Theological Seminary and having come to the West largely through Atkinson's influence; and Atkinson was strongly in favor of Congregationalist control. We have no way of knowing how much influence Sidney Marsh had in seeing that the acting presidency at the time of his death went to his brother the classicist, who favored nondenominational control, rather than to Lyman the scientist, who favored Congregationalist control, but both the choice and the ultimate outcome of that choice would have pleased him.

When the smoke cleared—or, as the trustees' minutes put it, "after prolonged review

Joseph Walker Marsh, hired in 1867 as professor of ancient languages, twice served as acting president during crucial transition periods and was influential in perpetuating Sidney Harper Marsh's vision of an autonomous liberal arts college. The two Marshes were half-brothers; when Sidney Marsh's mother, Lucia Wheelock Marsh, died, his father married her sister, who later became Joseph's mother. James Rood Robertson wrote of Joseph Marsh in 1905, when the latter was the oldest member of the faculty: "Character is the chief object to be attained according to his standards, and for forty years he has exemplified to his students the things he has taught."

John Russell Herrick, Pacific's second president, had the unenviable position of trying to fill Sidney Marsh's shoes. Though his tenure lasted only four years, Herrick accomplished a good deal, including raising the $16,000 required to erect "Ladies Hall," (1884) Pacific University's first dormitory for women (top), which would later bear his name (1887). At the opening ceremonies, Herrick delivered an address entitled "The Higher Education of Woman, the Last Chapter in the History of Liberty."

with very full and free discussion of the interests involved"—the man who emerged as Pacific's new president was Rev. John Herrick, who, as Robertson notes, "was even more opposed than President Marsh to anything that might be regarded as sectarian." Herrick—who, like Joseph Marsh and so many others associated with Pacific's early years, hailed from Vermont—was what we would today call an "ecumenical" Christian. One of his most ambitious and cherished goals as president of Pacific was to merge all of the Christian schools in the State of Oregon, regardless of denomination, into a single, large State University. The trustees, however, vigorously opposed such a radical concept, and Herrick would stay at Pacific for only four years, hardly long enough to bring them around.

Moreover, Herrick, like Marsh before him, was forced to spend much of his time in the East seeking patronage and funding—so much so that he never even managed to establish a home in Oregon. In spite of his short term and his enforced absenteeism, Herrick accomplished a good deal during his tenure, including the construction of "Ladies Hall," a new building that would later be renamed "Herrick Hall" (not to be confused with a still later building that would bear the same name). It was during Herrick's short reign as well, that Pacific, in collaboration with Captain M. C. Wilkinson of the U.S. Army, established an

industrial school for Indians. But when John Herrick left Pacific in 1883 to return to the East for good, the issue of sectarian control was still as hot as when he had assumed office four years earlier. It was about to get hotter.

STACKING THE DECK: PRESIDENT ELLIS

In contrast to the period following President Marsh's demise, the trustees, on Herrick's departure, acted swiftly. Instead of appointing a new president, however, they took the unprecedented step of creating the position of vice president and then offering it to Rev. Jacob Ellis, a native of Ohio and a graduate of Wheaton College. Though Ellis is routinely listed as president of Pacific University from 1883 to 1891, the minutes of the board clearly state that he served in the newly created position of vice president for the first three years, during which time, apparently, the institution was without a president. The reasons for this are not clear, but the tenor of the minutes suggests that it stemmed from divisiveness among the board members on the issue of "denominational relations."

Reverend Ellis arrived at Pacific University in 1883, the same year that the first transcontinental railroad arrived in Oregon, and for those loyal to Sidney Harper Marsh's vision of a non-sectarian college, the coincidence of these two events might well have seemed symbolic. Besides not being a New Englander, Ellis differed from his two predecessors in that his background was largely pastoral rather than pedagogical: he had come to Oregon as pastor of the Congregational Church at Forest Grove in 1875 and had left to take up a pastorate in Seattle before being called back to serve as vice president of Pacific.

Also, in contrast to either Sidney Marsh or John Herrick, Ellis seems to have had considerable sympathy with the sciences: he attempted, unsuccessfully, to establish an affiliation with a medical school in Portland, and he made significant changes in faculty and curriculum, including the addition of courses in such practical fields as applied chemistry and

Help From the Morse Brothers

WHEN SIDNEY HARPER MARSH needed to raise funds for Tualatin Academy and Pacific University, he relied heavily on assistance from faithful Congregationalists in New England. Among these loyal friends from the Atlantic seaboard were brothers Sidney and Samuel Morse. Their gifts to the fledgling college provided crucial operating support.

Samuel F. B. Morse is, of course, famous for his invention of the telegraph and Morse Code; his brother Sidney is less well known. Their father, Rev. Jedidiah Morse, was a Congregationalist pastor and an early American geographer—sometimes called the "Father of American Geography" because he authored the first geographical texts published in the United States at the start of the nineteenth century. When Sidney Morse donated 400 titles from his father's library—including many rare volumes from Europe—Pacific's library was the largest of any Oregon college. In 1880 the collection of 5,000 titles was twice as large as that of the closest rival, Willamette University in Salem.

In the 1870s, the famous inventor donated four telegraph instruments—two transmitters and two receivers—to the college, probably to be used as scientific apparatus. For many years these instruments were displayed in the library, but eventually went to the Pacific University Museum in Old College Hall.

In 1860, Samuel Morse lent his illustrious name to the following letter of introduction for President Marsh, leading to more support among Morse's friends and colleagues.

Librarian Shellie Slyter (third from right) shows Samuel F. Morse's original telegraph instruments and other library treasures to new students in September 1937.

No. 5 West 22. 1860

My dear Sir,

Permit me to introduce to you President Marsh of the Pacific University, at Forest Grove near Portland, Oregon.

Mr. Marsh will give you details in regard to this most important institution.

I have myself so strong a belief that no benevolent funds could be so well bestowed with the prospect of more widespread benefits not merely in that locality but also throughout the Pacific coast that I have most cheerfully given my mite to help build up this promising University.

Please think of this plan and if you can, in the enlarged benevolence of your nature, so ready to diffuse your wealth for great & good objects, encourage him by a donation, I feel assured you will. I know of no object at present, which promises a greater return in good fruit than the one here commended to your attention.

In haste but with Sincere esteem....

Sam. F. B. Morse

During the adminstration of President Ellis, courses in applied chemistry and assaying were added to the curriculum. Right: A chemistry laboratory in Science Hall (now Old College Hall) in the 1890s. This room is now an exhibit gallery in the Pacific University Museum. The original blackboard was discovered in the wall during extensive restoration in the 1970s and is visible in the gallery.

General O. O. Howard, 1875

General Oliver Otis Howard (1830-1909), sometimes called the "One-armed Christian Soldier" because of his Civil War injury and strong religious convictions, commanded U.S. Army troops in the Pacific Northwest (Department of the Columbia) from 1874-1879. Based at Ft. Vancouver on the Columbia River, Gen. Howard led the expedition against the Nez Perce Indians when Chief Joseph retreated to Canada in 1877. Howard's connections to the Congregational Church influenced the decision to establish an Indian Training School in Forest Grove, with ties to Pacific University. The school's first Superintendent, Lt. Melville Wilkinson, was Gen. Howard's personal assistant before assuming that role. Both men were active in the Portland YMCA.

Howard University, opened in Washington, D.C., in 1867 to educate freed slaves after the Civil War, was started by the First Congregational Society. They named the school for Gen. Howard because he was in charge of the post-war Freedman's Bureau.

assaying. That he uncompromisingly saw Pacific University as a religious institution, however, is clear from the motto that he selected for the college: "*Pro Christo et Regno Ejus*"— "For Christ and His Kingdom." And Christ's kingdom, in Ellis' view, was decidedly Congregational.

In 1889, George Atkinson died, and it was perhaps in memory of the former founder that Ellis judged the time to be ripe for affecting a change to strict Congregationalist control of the university—a miscalculation as it turned out. By now Ellis was president and had replaced many of the faculty who opposed him; he probably also had a hand in replacing Alanson Hinman, who had served as chair of the Board of Trustees since Sidney Harper Marsh's death, with George Shindler, who, unlike Hinman, shared Ellis' views.

On June 6, 1890, Shindler appointed a committee of the board to resolve "Denominational Relations." At the board meeting of June 20, the committee came back with a majority report, laced with quotes from the late George Atkinson, favoring Congregationalist control, and a minority report, with quotes from Sidney Harper Marsh, opposing it. On both reports, to Ellis' chagrin, the board split right down the middle—five for and five against—and the issue was tabled. Perhaps most surprising and galling to Ellis was the fact that among those opposing him was George Atkinson's son, Edward, who apparently placed personal convictions above loyalty to the memory of his father.

Before the June 20th meeting was over, George Shindler had resigned as chair of the board and Alanson Hinman was reappointed. Thwarted, Rev. Jacob Ellis straightway resigned as president and left Pacific, taking with him the larger part of the instructors whom he had recruited over his eight-year tenure. When the dust settled, only Joseph Marsh and William Ferrin—another native of Vermont, who would later serve as president for 13 years—remained of the original corps of instructors from Sidney Marsh's day. More to the point, the issue of sectarian control had still not been resolved.

A KIND OF SOLUTION: PRESIDENT McCLELLAND

On Ellis' departure, Joseph Marsh was once again appointed acting president until the board could find a replacement. It was probably clear to Marsh and everyone else by now that the only position to take on the thorny matter of sectarian control was one of compromise. What they needed was an able negotiator, and they found just that in the person of Rev. Thomas McClelland, a native of Ireland who had come to America as a child.

As we shall see, McClelland would ably man the helm of the university up to the turn of the century. His immediate task, however, was to ride out the waves of divisiveness that followed in the wake of Ellis' departure. Drawing on his considerable talents as an administrator, he led a movement to amend the charter so that two-thirds of the board should be Congregationalists, but elected by the board as the original charter had provided.

As Robertson reports: "Thus the institution

Alanson Hinman, left, served as chair of the Board of Trustees from 1879 until 1889, when President Ellis moved to replace him. He was reappointed to the chair in 1890. In total Hinman served on the Board for 52 years. Horace Lyman, right, a close friend of founder George Atkinson, was Pacific University's first faculty member, serving initially as professor of mathematics and later as chair of history and rhetoric. Lyman founded the First Congregational Church in Portland and, while at Pacific, periodically served as pastor of the Congregational Church in Forest Grove. When he died in 1887, at the age of 71, **The Oregonian** *praised him as "a man who performed every duty that life laid upon him with a cheerful and ready devotion."*

was enabled to retain the broad nonsectarian character which had been in the past emphasized, and at the same time secure the patronage of a denomination closely identified with educational institutions in the West." A further stipulation of the new charter was that Pacific University should never be removed from Forest Grove, a proposition that had been seriously entertained during the stormy Ellis years.

With the last founder gone and the question of the non-sectarian nature of the university more or less settled, the "pioneer" period of Pacific University comes to a close. Against tremendous odds and outright opposition, Sidney Harper Marsh's "one idea" had prevailed, an idea commemorated in the quotation from Marsh that graces the west wall of present-day Jefferson Hall: "It is intended that the study and instruction here given shall cultivate the power of right thinking, and ground the student in the principles of right action." For now at least, the "house that Marsh built" was standing firm.

The non-denominational nature of Pacific University withstood its most serious threat during the administration of Rev. Jacob "Frank" Ellis (1883–1891). Recruited by George Atkinson, Ellis put considerable energy into stacking the board and faculty with members sympathetic to Congregationalist control, a strategy that might have succeeded had Atkinson not died in the interim.

FOREST GROVE INDIAN TRAINING SCHOOL

*I*N 1879, during the administration of President John Herrick and largely through the efforts of Rev. George Atkinson, Pacific University set about to administer the only off-reservation boarding school for Indian children in the western United States. The Forest Grove Indian Training School was established a few blocks from the main university campus, roughly occupying the residential block now surrounded by 22nd and 23rd Avenues and C and D Streets. The first group of 18 students, from the Puyallup Indian Reservation near Tacoma, Washington, arrived in Forest Grove on February 25, 1880. For the next five years over 300 Indian students from Washington Territory, Oregon, Northern California, and Alaska attended the school. Relocated to Salem and renamed in early 1885, the Chemawa Indian School still operates the oldest off-reservation boarding school in the nation.

U.S. President Rutherford B. Hayes, during a trip to Portland, made a visit to Forest Grove in 1880 specifically to see the Indian Training School (the only time a sitting U.S. President ever came to town). The school, considered an innovative experiment at the time, also attracted the attention of the national press. At right is an excerpt from an article entitled "Indian Schools in Oregon," which appeared in *Harper's Weekly* in 1882. While the attitudes expressed may grate on our modern, and presumably more enlightened, sensibilities, the article is presented here without comment as an accurate record of how "thinking men" in the late nineteenth century struggled to come to grips with "The Indian Question."

[From *Harper's Weekly* (Vol. XXVI, No. 1327), 27 May 1882.]
FOREST GROVE, near Portland, Oregon, is the site of an Indian training school, where some very interesting and valuable educational work is going on. The institution is under the superintendence of Captain M.C. Wilkinson, U.S.A., to whose zeal, patience, and tact its success is entirely due. Like all thinking men who have been brought into relations with the aborigines of this continent, Captain Wilkinson has devoted much reflection to what is called the Indian question. He believes that the real solution of the problem lies in the systematic education of the rising generation. He is no advocate of that system of bribery and terror which has so long prevailed on the frontier, but asserts that the Indian tribal relations must be broken up as incompatible with our social organization, and that no adult member of any tribe be kept as a ward of the government. Let the adults provide for themselves, as the rest of us have to do. But in the case of the children Captain Wilkinson

The Forest Grove Indian Training School was home to over 300 Indian students between 1880 and 1885 before the school relocated to Salem and became the Chemawa Indian School. Photographer Isaac Davidson took a series of photographs at the school including these "before and after" images. The photo on the left bears the caption, "New recruits—Spokane Indians," and the one on the right, "New Recruits—after seven months at school." One student died in the interim.

justly holds that the government can with benefit to all parties expend its money in their education and training. They ought to be taught various trades and handicrafts, so that when they return to their homes they may be properly fitted for life's struggles, and will infuse new ambitions into future generations, and be missionaries of the higher life of order, labor, and civilization.

In the training school at Forest Grove one hundred young Indians between the ages of five and twenty are kept, well fed, well clothed, and happy, and, as far as can be judged from appearances, quite as intelligent as a similar number of white youths. They came to the school from the prairies and the mountains, dressed in blankets and moccasins, with uncut and unkempt hair, as wild as young coyotes. They have already learned to sing like nightingales and work like beavers. It is remarkable that these young children of the forest are perfectly amenable to discipline, and never break a rule. The boys learn how to make boots and shoes, build houses, shoe horses, and how to perform the various operations of agriculture. The girls learn to sew, darn, wash, cook, churn, iron, wash dishes, and keep their rooms in order. Both sexes learn their lessons promptly, and retain what they learn tenaciously. The common school games and amusements, playing ball, running races, and the like, are indulged in by the boys, while the little girls play with their dolls. They attend religious meetings and lectures, and sing and pray. The singing, indeed, is of remarkable excellence.

Captain Wilkinson last fall conducted his dusky pupils on a visit to Portland to attend the Young Men's Christian Association meeting, and the sight of these young red-skins excited general admi-

ration. Captain Wilkinson gave some details of the organization of the school. The United States government for the first year appropriated only $5000 for him to start a school of twenty-five pupils, furnish transportation for them, teach, board, and house them. The boys built the houses themselves, the government only furnishing the materials. The four acres assigned to the institution were cultivated by the boys, who grubbed up the stumps, and planted potatoes and vegetables for their table. The school is thus partly self-supporting. The boys are attired in a regular uniform, and have their regular officers, as in our military schools. Every advantage placed in their way is eagerly seized on by these pupils, and it is worthy of notice by those who talk of the incorrigible character of the Indians that the parents, many of them chiefs, willingly and thankfully surrendered their sons and daughters in order that they might be taught the arts and learning of the white man. ...

We agree with Captain Wilkinson that this is the best solution of the difficulty which confronts us in our dealings with the Indians. The present race, demoralized by our vacillating and inconsistent Indian policy, may perhaps deserve the reputation of being incorrigible; let us then take the rising generation away from the evil influences which have surrounded their progenitors, and train them up to be useful and orderly members of society.

The top photograph has the caption: "One of the Main Buildings, erected entirely by Indian Boys; Dormer Windows, Rustic and Painting on all.—Their work without aid."

The lower photograph is captioned "Shoemaking" and was used as the basis for an illustration accompanying the Harper's Weekly *article reprinted here. The instructor, Samuel Walker, is the father of Charles Walker ('06), for whom Walker Hall was named.*

Left: A button from an Indian School uniform. The button was designed by Dr. Henry Minthorn, superintendent after Captain Wilkinson, in 1883.

ACT II

From College to University

1891-1945

The McClelland Decade:
Emergence of a Modern College

With the ignorance which characterizes Americans as to other regions than their own, I very much underestimated both the field and the work. — REV. THOMAS MCCLELLAND, 1892

GEORGE ATKINSON'S death in 1889 marked the end of an era for Pacific University. After 40 years of bare existence, the long, upward climb toward true collegiate status had ended. The final decade of the nineteenth century witnessed changes that would shape the very nature and identity of the school. A number of traditions and practices woven into the fabric of the university, and some associated with college life in general, began during the 1890s. In essence, Pacific became what we think of as a modern college. One individual, the Rev. Thomas McClelland (1846–1926), played a key role during the time he served as Pacific's fourth president, 1891–1900. In almost every sense, the 1890s at Pacific University were the "McClelland Decade."

HEALING OLD WOUNDS, BREAKING NEW GROUND

When, following the sinking of the *Maine* in 1898, the United States declared war on Spain, a Madrid newspaper reported that "The Commander-in-Chief of the American Army is one Ted Roosevelt, formerly a New York policeman" who had been "born near Haarlem" but had "emigrated to America when young," who had been educated at "Harvard Academy, a commercial school," and who now went about the country accompanied by a bodyguard of toughs fittingly known as "rough rioters."

As amusing as these misconceptions are, the impressions that most Americans had of what was going on out in Oregon in the 1890s were hardly more accurate—a fact noted by President McClelland in his inaugural address, cited above. Thus in 1894 the president of the University of Rochester, in a similar address, took aim at "fresh water [sic] colleges away out in the far west":

> I can remember the day when … it seemed to be the regular thing for the student to exercise his wits and to show his ability by playing practical jokes upon his professors and especially upon the other classes. This state of things is passing away and only is now present … where the academy characteristics prevail, where they take the students while they are young before their eyes are opened to the world … in some frontier place where they would give to the institutions a higher name than college if there were any.

The barb was both uninformed and gratuitous, and out in the far West the student edi-

Pacific's fourth president, Thomas McClelland

Index *Staff, 1902*

Interestingly, his vita reads like a patchwork of his three most influential predecessors at Pacific University: like Harvey Clark, he studied at Ohio's liberal Oberlin College, receiving a degree of A.B. in 1875; like Marsh, he continued his formal education at Union Theological Seminary in New York; like George Atkinson, he ultimately graduated from Andover Theological Seminary in Massachusetts. Following 11 years as professor of philosophy at Tabor College in Iowa, he came to Forest Grove to take on the administrative responsibilities as Pacific's president.

McClelland's influence was immediate and pervasive. Besides resolving the conflict about Congregational control, he was responsible for bringing to Pacific at least two faculty members who would play significant roles long after his departure—Henry Liberty Bates and Mary Frances Farnham, of whom we shall see more later. In 1892, eight years after Ladies Hall had begun providing on-campus housing for female students, McClelland gave male students their first opportunity to live communally in one of the former Indian Training School buildings, renamed the "Boys Dormitory." In 1893, he further bolstered Pacific's reputation as an innovative school by introducing for the first time an elective system—this while other colleges in the region retained prescribed curricula. The morale of the school blossomed under his administration, as did community pride in the institution. In 1893, by city ordinance, the streets bordering the university were renamed—Pacific Avenue and College Way.

Several other factors contributed to the positive changes at the university during McClelland's tenure, the most important being Portland's economic and cultural flowering. Since the completion of the Northern Pacific Railroad in 1883, the population had more than doubled, bringing with it to the region contemporary ideas about education. Pacific University, although located on the Portland fringe, nevertheless benefited from this growth, not least of all because greatly improved roads had transformed Forest Grove

tor of Pacific University's fledgling newspaper bristled that "this slur should be cast on western colleges":

> To the schools of the west belongs the credit of bringing about this reformation in the college world. Founded by men who were teaching for the good they could do and not for the money they might receive, the early western institutions drew to themselves students who were in earnest, who were intent on an education and had neither time nor inclination for the age-dusted tricks with which eastern college boys kept green the memory of forerunners whose atoning studiousness they entirely disregarded …
> the few fossils yet remaining are on the Atlantic coast.

As insignificant as this exchange of volleys might seem, it bears testimony to the fact that Pacific University, by the mid-1890s, had acquired not only a college newspaper but a great deal of college pride. Both of these acquisitions were due in great part to the work of Rev. Thomas McClelland.

Thomas McClelland was born in Ireland, in County Derry, and emigrated to Pennsylvania with his large family—he was the youngest of 13 children—at the age of three. Ten years later, in 1859, his family moved to Mendon, Illinois. When the Civil War started, he was too young to enlist, but saw his older brothers go off to serve in the Union Army.

from an outpost to something of a suburb. On almost every front—academics, athletics, social organizations, publications—student life began to take on the pace and appearance of the "modern" college.

THE SEEDS OF TRADITION

Two of the longest-standing traditions among student activities began during the McClelland decade: the student newspaper, called the *Index,* in January of 1893; and the yearbook, called *The Heart of Oak,* in the following year. Taken together, the *Index* and *The Heart of Oak* provide a long-running commentary on campus life at Pacific University from the students' vantage.

There is no record of who came up with the name "Index," though the first editor-in-chief, H. D. Stewart of the class of 1893, notes by way of explanation that the paper "should serve as an index to the plane of thought of the students which it represents." Two years later a sophomore editor-in-chief named P. E. Bauer apparently felt that the name was sufficiently unimaginative to warrant something of an apology:

> INDEX means the "pointer" and that is what we intend to be. We will point out the advantage of PACIFIC UNIVERSITY wherever we see it, give points on athletics and pointers about students, also make the editorials as pointed as possible. Even the type used is on the point system.

Whatever the virtues of the newspaper's moniker, the editors of the *Index* clearly took their responsibilities as pioneer chroniclers seriously. The second issue—February 1893—includes an accounting of the newly formed "rugby football" team's record "so that it may be preserved as a matter of history in the development of our athletics." Noting that Pacific's first football game ever was "played after only three or four weeks of practice," and that only "three or four students had any knowledge of the game at that time," the article goes on to a present the line-up for both teams and a summary of the action, which took

place on the grounds on the north side of the college campus. The opposition was the Bishop Scott Academy team, which, it is noted, had been playing for two or three years:

> The visitors having had considerable experience in the game, led off with strong and rapid playing and succeeded in scoring the first touch down. After this the home team began to realize what it meant to play football, and started in to win, with the result that the game ended with a score of 18 to 6 in favor of Pacific University.

The perils of rugby football, which included serious head injuries due to the lack of helmets of any kind, was apparently a hot issue nationally and becomes a recurrent theme in the Index throughout the 1890s. The March

Top: Boys' Dormitory and Club of 1897; the building was originally constructed for the Forest Grove Indian Training School.

Bottom: A room in Herrick Hall at the turn of the century illustrated the contemporary Victorian fashion in fabrics and furnishings. Ladies Hall was renamed Herrick Hall in 1897.

The 1899 football team (showing some players wearing nose guards) poses in an "action" shot outside Marsh Hall.

Right: At the "Annual Banquet" at the turn of the century, Boxer (see p. 61) puts in an appearance. Far right: The Ivy Club of 1891

The actors in a play pose for the camera (ca. 1900). Far right: Various University pins showing an early version of the University Seal and also one with T.A. for Tualatin Academy.

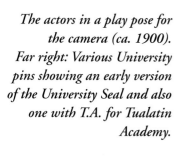

Music at Pacific

ACIFIC'S FIRST PRESIDENT, Sidney Harper Marsh, peppered his letters home with reminders to his children to keep up on their music lessons and to practice regularly. Marsh considered music an essential component of a truly liberal education, and the tradition he fostered has continued at Pacific to this day.

Pacific University offered its first music courses as early as 1870, nine years before Marsh's death. The catalog for 1870–71 lists Miss Olivia Haskell as Teacher of Music in the Faculty roster. Miss Haskell came to Forest Grove armed with a degree from Oberlin College's Conservatory of Music. Forty years later, this same Miss Haskell worked as the matron of Herrick Hall, keeping a close watch on the female residents of that beloved dormitory.

Gradually, the course offerings in music expanded until, in 1884, the Conservatory of Music was formally created, with Mary H. Edwards serving as director. Until 1902 a total of six women worked as conservatory directors. In that milestone year, Frank Thomas Chapman arrived at Pacific, with distinguished credentials from Europe, to take charge of the conservatory. His wife, Pauline Miller Chapman, was employed as the head of the vocal department. During the first decade of this century the Chapmans shaped and improved the Conservatory of Music on campus. The 1913 *Heart of Oak* noted that the Pacific University Conservatory of Music "is now acknowledged one of the best conservatories in the Northwest and the standards of requirement are on a par with those of the best, both in America and on the continent." Chapman Hall, a small house formerly used for music classes, was named in honor of Frank and Pauline Chapman.

The Conservatory of Music continued to grow in prestige and stature throughout the first half of the twentieth century. In the World War II period, however, the music program at Pacific experienced a change, and the conservatory—a vestige of nineteenth century academic structure—was discontinued and replaced by the Department of Music. After five years, in 1950, the official School of Music appeared in the university catalog. Under the new administrative arrangement, it operated on a parallel level with the College of Arts and Sciences and the College of Optometry, using the title of "dean" for the school's director. The School of Music, based in Knight Hall, maintained this separate identity until 1983, when the music program, once again, was absorbed into the College of Arts and Sciences.

Limited facilities hampered the growth of the music program at Pacific University for most of its life. For many years two historic structures—both houses constructed in the nineteenth century by President Sidney Harper Marsh—provided inadequate space for the School of Music during its prime. This situation came close to changing for the better in 1970, when Pacific acquired the old Lincoln Junior High School building adjacent to campus (where the Holce Tennis Courts are now located). Plans to move the School of Music into this structure were foiled, however, when the building caught fire and burned.

Music students and faculty rejoiced in 1993 when the new Taylor-Meade Performing Arts Center opened. This long-awaited addition has filled a void not only on campus but within the Forest Grove community as a whole. Within the center, the 400-seat McCready Auditorium is the venue for the annual Stars in the Grove event and for other locally popular musical performances.

Ken Combs, the last dean of the School of Music (1978–1983) and director of planning when the Taylor-Meade Performing Arts Center was being envisioned, attributed the continuing interest in music at Pacific to the excellence of the music faculty. "Some musicians can perform," Combs noted, "but can't teach. Pacific's faculty are good performers and good teachers."

"Mr. Wilderness"

Olaus J. Murie

THE NAME OLAUS J. MURIE is well known to anyone with an interest in natural history or wildlife conservation. Murie's book, *A Field Guide to Animal Tracks,* published in 1954 for the famous Peterson Field Guide Series, graces many bookshelves. Less well known is that this internationally recognized wilderness advocate and conservation leader graduated from Pacific University in 1912. While at Pacific, Murie served as class president during both his junior and senior years and was active in several campus clubs. He also played on the football team, ran track as a member of the eight-mile relay team, and contributed many humorous illustrations to the 1913 *Heart of Oak* (published in 1912).

In April 1953, Murie returned to Pacific to deliver three lectures for the Isaac Hillman Lectureships in the Social Sciences under the general topic of "Wild Country as a National Asset." One lecture title in particular reflects his views on wilderness in America: "God Bless America—And Let's Save Some of It!"

The following passage from one of Murie's lectures presents a good student assessment of life at Pacific, one that transcends the period to which it refers.

I should like to talk for a moment about Pacific University and my experience with it. For me it has seemed a happy coincidence that I should have the opportunity to visit this university and talk about wilderness and what it means for us. In the first place, we can be proud of the origin of this college, over a century ago, in the pioneering period of this land. This institution was really the beginning of education in Oregon. It speaks for the vision of early pioneers in thought, who foresaw what would be the ultimate need.

I like to recall my own introduction to this historic place, though some of my first experiences on this campus are ludicrous to me now. I came to Pacific as a sophomore in 1909. I had grown up in flat Minnesota country and had worked mostly as a farm hand. Then for three days and nights I had sat in a day coach of the Northern Pacific, with a basket of food beside me, for I could not afford to buy meals enroute. I had never seen a mountain, hardly a sizeable hill. Consider then what it meant to be crossing the Rocky Mountains! Then came the lush valley and the great forests of this very place.

As time went on I came to appreciate more fully the particular quality of life at Pacific University. I know that I cannot properly analyze this. I found here a charming countryside, and back there on the ridges was the deep forest in the condition that Lewis and Clark might have found it. As I look back, it seems to me we had a little community culture that was precious in a special way. It was close to the land. It had tranquillity, so priceless in the world today. Perhaps our facilities were not what they should be; perhaps even some of our courses were not as "strong" as we have them now. Yet here in the edge of wilderness, born of the wilderness, was an institution where, from the vantage point of an atmosphere of simplicity and serenity, we could form our opinions of the strivings of mankind.

When Olaus Murie died in 1963, an editorial in the *Washington Post* summed up the common opinion that "to thousands of people who had hiked or camped with Olaus J. Murie or had talked with him on a mountain trail, he was Mr. Wilderness."

1893 issue cites the opinion of "the venerable Ex-President of Princeton College," who had called for a national conference of college presidents, professors, and parents of students "to consider how benefits may be secured from manly exercises without the accompanying evils."

As for womanly exercises, an editorial in the April 1893 issue observes:

> We are glad to notice the enthusiasm with which lawn tennis is being taken up this season by the students. It is the only outdoor game which we have that can be entered into by women with the same degree of propriety as by men, and for this reason, if no other, it should always retain a prominent position among college games.

Other sports on campus that began during the McClelland decade included baseball, basketball, and track (women's basketball and track teams started competing at the close of the decade, in 1899). It was during this period as well that the school colors—crimson and black—were chosen, a fact duly commemorated in the October 1894 issue of the *Index* in this anonymous bit of acrostic verse:

ROUGE ET NOIR
The colors of our college
Are black
& crimson-red
Pilfered from my maiden's cheek and the hair
Upon her head.

The same issue contains a spirited defense of the school's initials, P.U., which had of late been pirated by the upstart student body of Portland University. Under the headline "What's in A Name?" the article proclaims that "The best colleges in the country recognize P. U. degrees and the desire of our founders has been attained—they have builded [sic] on this North Pacific coast an institution of higher learning whose standing is equal to the New England colleges from which they came." The writer concludes in a burst of gratuitous Latin and questionable grammar: "To borrow our time-honored *nomina duogrammata* and ap-

ply it to a school of later origin is to obtain for that school's students a consideration to which they are not entitled, have not yet earned, to obtain it under false pretenses." Apparently, the high seriousness of the editorial achieved its end; the following issue of the *Index* notes that "The students of the Portland University have very generously, in deference to Pacific's prior claims to the initials P. U., decided hereafter to use only the letter 'P' to represent their college."

Student life at Pacific in the 1890s was varied and lively, and most of it finds its way into the *Index* in one way or another. Debating, even more than athletics, was the main arena for competition with other schools. Christian activities of various kinds were conducted under the aegis of the YMCA and YWCA. There were clubs for everything from archery to bicycling to drama. And music, in the form of orchestra, band, glee clubs, chamber groups, and even "Mongolian mandolin accompaniments," played a central role in public events from the smallest tea party to the grandest ceremony. Dancing would not be permitted on campus until the 1920s, though female students were known to dance with one another at socials held in Ladies Hall.

In May of 1894 the *Index* announced the imminent publication of the "Annual," which it describes as "a veritable Pacific picture book—college life in all its forms." The premier issue of the *Heart of Oak*—a name suggested for the yearbook by Henry Liberty Bates in recognition of the many majestic oaks on the campus—appeared the following June and opens with a proud volley, announcing itself as "the

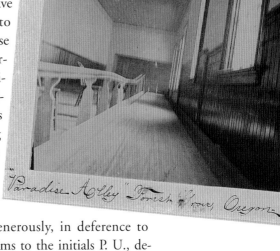

"Paradise Alley," the one-lane bowling alley in Marsh Hall in 1901

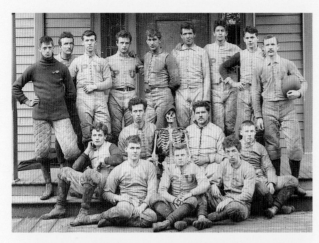

Top: The football team of 1894 included a skeleton in their team photos. When a photo later appeared in the Heart of Oak *yearbook the skeleton had been removed by a retoucher—a shadow of the skeleton's left shoulder is still visible.*

Four women with the "Petrified Stump" (ca. 1905)

first Annual ever issued on the North Pacific Coast." The student-writer, however, almost immediately assumes a more modest tone, couched in prose reminiscent of Joseph Addison, the seventeenth-century British essayist, considered at the time to be the apex of literary journalism:

> We publish it for our own amusement. If others find amusement in it we shall be doubly paid. It is not intended to be the instrument of any great good, but we hope it is sufficiently free from evil features that wherever it goes it will bear no blighting influence.

We have no tenets to set forth, no dogmas to maintain. We do not wish to offer any new policy for school management, or to attack any existing one. If such were needed it is not our mission. It is our purpose to give a simple view of Pacific University as it is. If in doing so we touch someone's pet notion or mention a peculiar trait, let him remember that he is only mortal and possibly may have inherited something of the human from his barbarian ancestors.

Despite this auspicious beginning, however, would-be editors of the annual proved to be "only mortal" as well. The *Heart of Oak* did not come out again until 1901, after which it appeared only sporadically until the 1920s, when it could truly be called a "yearbook." By contrast, the *Index*—first a monthly, then a weekly, currently a biweekly—has continued uninterrupted from its first issue to the present day.

Two other traditional figures familiar to Pacific alumni also date their origins to the McClelland decade: the petrified stump, which still marks the location of Tualatin Academy's log building, and Pacific's most enduring mascot, the bronze statue known as "Boxer." The stump, an unusual landmark by any standard, was erected in 1897 by the three alumni from the class of 1867. One of those graduates, Rev. Joseph Elkanah Walker, was also responsible for bringing "Boxer" to campus in 1898.

(Originally, the Chinese incense burner was known as "College Spirit"; the name "Boxer," a reference to the Boxer Rebellion, was coined by the *Index* staff in 1908.) While serving as a missionary to China, Rev. Walker bought the statue and sent it to his mother, who in turn donated it to Pacific. Boxer managed to stay on display for only a year before the first student "theft" literally launched it into its more active role in campus life, one that it would maintain for many years to come.

FITTING TRIBUTE

Perhaps the crowning achievement of McClelland's administration was the construction of Marsh Memorial Hall, named in honor of Pacific's first president. When McClelland arrived at Pacific, the campus consisted of only three structures—College Hall, Academy Hall, and Ladies Hall. What it lacked was a visual anchor in the form of a central, solid building.

Marsh Memorial Hall, designed by the noted Portland firm of Whidden and Lewis, would provide just such a landmark and put Forest Grove on the architectural map.

With plans in hand and a generous donation of $15,000 from Dr. D. K. Pearsons of Chicago in the bank, President McClelland and the trustees had every reason to hope for a speedy completion of the building. The groundbreaking ceremony, accompanied by appropriate fanfare, occurred during commencement of 1893, with Joseph and Eliza Marsh, the former president's brother and widow, throwing out the first two shovelfuls of dirt. But a less propitious event of national import was in the offing. A week after the groundbreaking, on June 27, the New York stock market crashed, setting off the second-greatest depression in United States history. The timing seemed ominous and, as it turned out, the laying of the cornerstone for Marsh

Above: The bronze statue known as "Boxer" was given to Pacific in 1898 by Rev. Joseph Elkanah Walker. Below: The community gathers to celebrate the laying of the cornerstone for Marsh Hall in June 1894 during commencement. Just prior to this event College Hall was relocated and renamed "Science Hall."

D. K. Pearsons of Chicago (a classmate of George Atkinson's at Dartmouth) donated $15,000 toward the construction of Marsh Hall and later offered to increase his gift to $50,000 if the University could raise $100,000 within a year.

Above, right: Members of the first class to enter Marsh Hall in the fall of 1895

This cup illustrating the Temperance Movement belonged to Tabitha Brown. Included in the contents of the Marsh Hall cornerstone box was a statement of Forest Grove's position on temperance.

Memorial Hall was delayed until the commencement of the following year.

In the meantime, in March of 1894, D. K. Pearsons offered to increase his gift of $15,000 for the building to $50,000 if the university could come up with $100,000 in pledges within a year. This would have been a Herculean task in the best of times; in the trough of a financial crash, it seemed impossible. Still, everyone pitched in to meet the unlikely deadline. President McClelland canvassed Oregon and traveled to the East Coast to solicit funds; the faculty, whose own salaries had not been paid in full, pledged $1,200; the alumni promised $7,000; and the trustees held themselves responsible for another $30,000. Bolstered by this initial response and by sheer faith, McClelland, still in the East drumming up support, gave the go-ahead for the laying of the cornerstone, which took place in June of 1894.

In McClelland's absence, Joseph Marsh conducted the ceremony, which was marked by appropriate speeches and, of course, music. Before Eliza Marsh set the stone in place, a potpourri of articles was deposited in a metal cornerstone box, including a copy of Sidney Harper Marsh's inaugural address, copies of the *Index* and the *Heart of Oak,* a list of donors, a statement of Forest Grove's position on temperance, a cone of "Douglas spruce" (presumably Douglas fir), three U.S. coins, and a copy of the *Oregonian* (Harvey Scott, Pacific's first graduate, was editor of the *Oregonian* at the time). The cache also included two photo-

graphs, one of Tabitha Brown and—an interesting touch—one of Mrs. Whidden, wife of the architect.

In spite of the fanfare and the heroic efforts to meet Dr. Pearsons' challenge, however, New Year's Day of 1895 found the total pledges considerably below the amount that was due in March. Then, on the morning of February 15, 1895, a group of students were seen putting up signs that read: "All students are requested to come to the mass meeting this evening in the college chapel." Beneath this, in large letters, was the addendum: "FACULTY ARE POSITIVELY NOT ALLOWED." The following morning a similar meeting was called, which lasted from nine until noon. The outcome of these two meetings was a pledge from the Pacific University student body of $4,065—an impressive figure indeed when we consider that total enrollment in the collegiate department at the time was 22.

An editorial in the February 1895 issue of the *Index* proudly hailed this achievement as one that would "prove more far-reaching … than anything which has ever before happened in the history of Pacific University":

The fact that the students voluntarily, and without the solicitation or even the knowledge of the faculty, have pledged themselves to pay upwards of four thousand dollars to the Pearsons fund … tells in unmistakable language how highly the students appreciate the advantages which they enjoy. It means that the men and women who have devoted their lives to laying the foundation and rearing the superstructure of this institution have not lived in vain. More than this, it means that the present administration of the university meets with the hearty approval of all the students, and what higher recommendation can any institution have than that the students like it?

Failing and Corbett: Mainstays of Pacific's Early Years

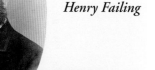

Henry Failing

HENRY FAILING (1834–1898) served as treasurer for Pacific's Board of Trustees for 28 years, from 1870 until his death in 1898. He came to Portland with his parents in 1851 and soon afterward opened a store with his father. Failing became a prominent business and civic leader, serving as Portland's mayor and president of the First National Bank.

In 1871 he joined his brother-in-law, Henry Corbett (1827–1903), who at the time was a U.S. Senator from Oregon, in a mercantile business that added to their collective wealth. Corbett also served on the Board of Trustees for Pacific University, from 1858 to 1903, and, in fact, preceded Failing as treasurer for a short time during the Civil War period. Few names could rival theirs in Portland's elite upper class during the nineteenth century.

Pacific's survival during the early years was in large part due to the business acumen of Henry Failing and Henry Corbett. In spite of their years of dedication and service to Pacific University, it is curious that neither man left a sizable bequest to increase the endowment or construct additional buildings.

Henry Winslow Corbett

Life in Forest Grove 1902

George Coghill was professor of biology, 1902-06.

Excerpt from: *George Ellett Coghill: Naturalist and Philosopher* by C. Judson Herrick.

THE FIRST OPENING was as professor of biology in Pacific University, at Forest Grove, Oregon, a small college with an honorable record as one of the pioneers of education in the far Northwest. The salary was $1,000 per year, payable as and when money was available; the duties were onerous and the equipment insignificant. Here the family was so poor that in the first season there was not enough money to buy postage stamps for Christmas cards. Mrs. Coghill gives some glimpses into the hardships of this pioneer life:

George borrowed money to go to Europe. When he returned we were broke. We borrowed $300.00 more to get us to our first job in Oregon with our ten-months-old baby. We moved into an empty seven-room house, after buying a cooking stove, kitchen table, dining table, four chairs, and iron bed and a canvas cot. Our dresser was two packing cases curtained under a mirror. George's 'study' had a pint-size airtight wood stove, a kitchen table, one wooden chair and again packing cases for books. George and I were almost down and out when we landed in Forest Grove. The sky was orange with smoke from forest fires, dust and ashes were everywhere, and our throats and eyes parched and sore. The quarterly salary payments were always spent before received. The village merchant, Mr. Adams, carried the whole faculty on his books six months of every year. In his store was a soft outing flannel that I wanted so much for night clothes for all of us—but no money. Mr. Adams asked, 'How much do you want?' I said, 'Oh, not any now.' He understood and replied, 'The whole faculty live on credit in this town. You'd better join up. They'll pay by Christmas.' But they didn't. By Christmas we did have sleeping garments, but no money for a postage stamp.

In further acknowledgment of the students' generosity, it was decreed that the date of February 15 should be celebrated in perpetuity as "Students' Day." History, sadly, has not done well by Students' Day. The first anniversary was celebrated with appropriate games and activities, but in the following year the catalog calendar would change the date to October 17 and would rename the holiday "Founders' Day." The reason given for the changed date was that February 15 was too close both to the end of winter term and to Washington's birthday. The name was changed because the faculty had always wanted to have a Founders' Day and did not feel that they could institute two new holidays. Consequently, the two holidays were collapsed into one, with the assurance, however, that "the day should still belong to the students for promoting their interests." Predictably, the origin of "Founders' Day," along with the assurance, was gradually forgotten.

Perhaps inspired by the students' gesture, Dr. Pearsons kindly extended the deadline to July 1898, which coincided with the 50th anniversary celebration of the school's founding. With generous local contributions adding to the sum, the university was able to raise $111,000 by the deadline—$11,000 over the required amount.

By this time, however, Marsh Hall was already three years old. It had been completed within two years of the groundbreaking and proudly dedicated on September 27, 1895. The original building held 13 classrooms, a library, administrative offices, and a chapel. Though gutted by a fire in 1975, it was completely restored within two years and stands today as a fitting tribute both to its namesake and to the spirit that permeated Pacific University during the McClelland decade.

END OF DECADE AND A CENTURY

The culminating event of President McClelland's administration was Pacific's 50th anniversary celebration in July 1898. Using 1848 as the founding date—the year that the Board of Trustees initially met—the semi-centennial highlighted the growth and development of Pacific University and Tualatin Academy. The event was attended by about 600 guests from Portland and beyond, including representatives from Whitman College, the University of Vermont, Carlton College, and Iowa College. Also present were numerous prominent members of the Council of Congregational Churches, which happened to be holding its national convention in Portland that year. Pacific University was on the map, and President McClelland's untiring efforts on its behalf had helped put it there.

At the close of both the decade and the century, however, Thomas McClelland bid farewell to Forest Grove. He stated his reasons in a letter written shortly after his departure:

> I had begun to feel the strain of the constant canvass for money at such a great distance from home and I was keenly sensible to the fact that under the circumstances I could not do for the institution all that, in my judgment, a president should do for a college.

On leaving Pacific, he took on the presidency of Knox College in Galesburg, Illinois. He

Brighton Chapel in Marsh Hall

would hold that position for 17 years, concluding a long and distinguished career in education. He died in Galesburg on January 26, 1926.

When McClelland left in 1900, there were six buildings on campus. Student enrollment was 50 in the university, more than double that of his inaugural year, and about 175 in the academy. There were 13 faculty members, a small number of instructors, and a curriculum that included a four-year classical program, a three-year scientific program, a three-year set of literary courses, and electives in music and art. Overall, though several Pacific University presidents served longer terms than Thomas McClelland, few did more to shape the essential character of the institution.

McClelland's influence on the development of Pacific University did not end with his departure in 1900. When steel millionaire Andrew Carnegie formed the Carnegie Foundation in 1905, he named Thomas McClelland to the Board of Directors. When, a year later, the first Herrick Hall (Ladies Hall) caught fire and burned to the ground, the Carnegie Foundation provided $10,000 for the new women's dormitory, constructed in 1907—this in addition to the $20,000 it had already promised in 1905 for the construction of a new library. McClelland surely had a hand in this.

On the less positive side, McClelland also had a hand in choosing his successor. When the trustees haggled for almost two years over who should succeed him as president, McClelland wrote back in no uncertain terms recommending William Ferrin for the job: "You speak of the difficulties of finding a president. I have been very firm in the conviction that Prof. Ferrin is the man for the place … Dr. Pearsons [of Pearsons' Fund fame] has two or three different times expressed very decidedly his conviction that Prof. Ferrin ought to be elected president." The trustees, reluctantly, took the advice and hired Ferrin, a decision that they would live to regret. In the next 13 years, over 30 of the faculty — including most of those carefully and judiciously recruited by McClelland — would resign in protest over the administrative style of William Ferrin.

This 1901 photo shows Academy Hall in the foreground and Marsh Hall. The classical entrance was added in 1900-1901. Academy Hall burned to the ground in 1910.

Last Class: Tualatin Academy and Beyond

Pacific belongs indeed to that important class of "the small" college and she is not only proud of it but is inclined to believe that her special mission to humanity is best fulfilled in that capacity.

— HENRY LIBERTY BATES

$\mathscr{T}$HE YEAR 1893, which saw so many other milestones in Pacific's history, also marks the end of a long-running administrative feud between Tualatin Academy and Pacific University. The central reason for this improvement was President McClelland's recruitment of Henry Liberty Bates in 1893 as principal of the academy and, four years later, of Mary Frances Farnham as principal of the Ladies Department. Both of these administrator-teachers served the academy well until it closed in 1915, after which they went on to become two of the most influential faculty members in Pacific University's history. Together, they contributed a combined total of 60 years of service; both died at the advanced age of 96.

A "DEFECT IN THE ORGANIZATION"

As noted in the last chapter, Thomas McClelland arrived to a campus in the throes of ideological and administrative turmoil, and on more than one front. The clash between sectarian and non-sectarian factions of Pacific University certainly dominated the scene on his arrival, but there was yet another cause of friction and confusion that we have yet to discuss—namely, the administrative tension between Tualatin Academy and Pacific University.

In his inaugural address, Sidney Marsh had proudly proclaimed: "The Academy has become the college." This, in fact, was not the case, though it remains a common misconception. Tualatin Academy did not turn into Pacific University, nor did they have any legal existence as separate institutions. In 1854, the Board of Trustees amended the charter of Tualatin Academy to include a "collegiate department" called "Pacific University," of which

Marsh became the first president. Strictly speaking, then, the academy was divided into two departments, the "collegiate" and what was sometimes referred to as the "preparatory," the latter having by far the lion's share of the students even up to 1915, when it closed. During the McClelland decade, for example, enrollment in the collegiate department ranged from a low of 18 (1890–91) to a high of 52

Academy Hall was destroyed by fire in 1910. It stood close to the present site of Trombley Square (opposite).

(1899–1900), while enrollment in the preparatory department during the same period ranged from 92 (1890–91) to 176 (1899–1900).

The matter was further complicated by the fact that the preparatory department also included the "Ladies Department," which had its own principal. To sum up, the academy as a whole had a principal, while one of the departments within the academy had its own principal, and another department, which was called a "university," had a president. This organizational structure, it is worth noting, was concocted by the same Board of Trustees that came up with the name "Forest Grove," an oxymoron at best. (Marsh, perhaps recognizing this, always referred to Forest Grove as simply "The Grove.")

Above: Henry Liberty Bates
Below: Bates and President
Thomas McClelland in front
of Marsh Hall

Such an arrangement was almost bound to generate a good deal of administrative tension. Sidney Harper Marsh had referred to this conflict in his already-cited speech to the trustees in 1878:

The evil, generally pretty well understood by the Academy Principal and myself, grew more incorrigible just in proportion as the College work expanded and tended to draw the Academy into a subordinate relation. I have not space to show the complications caused by such defect in the organization. Men of affairs, and especially College men, may imagine the probable consequence. The public did not understand it, while it was the subtile [sic] and occult cause of outward difficulties.

While the "defect in the organization" was never resolved, the "outward difficulties" virtually dissolved with the arrival on campus of Henry Liberty Bates. Hand-picked by Thomas McClelland in 1893, Bates had been a long-time friend and classmate of the president. They had attended Oberlin College together, they had been ordained Congregational pastors together, and, sharing the Progressive Era philosophy of education, they would work together as a dynamic team, initiating more fundamental changes in the overall institution than had ever been witnessed before and, probably, since. At no other time in Tualatin Academy's history, certainly, would there be a more congenial relationship between the leaders of the respective "departments."

"PRIN BATES"

Henry Liberty Bates—or "Prin Bates" as he was affectionately known by the students—had been born January 7, 1853 near Akron, Ohio. He obtained his A.B. degree from Oberlin in 1876 and, for the next two years, taught school in Kelleys Island, Ohio and Keokuk, Iowa. Bates returned to the Oberlin Theological Seminary to prepare himself for the ministry, finishing the course of study in 1881. His first pastorate led him to Dover, Ohio, but his next callings took him further afield—first to Seattle, Washington, then to Petaluma, California, and fi-

nally to Eugene, Oregon. It was from Eugene, at President McClelland's request, that Henry Bates came to Forest Grove.

As principal of Tualatin Academy, Bates worked closely with President McClelland on all fronts. He also assisted with coaching athletics; photos of the Maurice Thompson Archery Club show Henry Liberty Bates proudly standing among the other members, bow in hand. Few areas of endeavor escaped his influence or his attention; the Pacific University Archives contains scrapbooks kept by Bates, covering every detail of campus life from 1893 through 1926. Not included is any reference to a personal tragedy in 1895, when Bates' wife of only 10 years, Cora Nichols Bates, died. They had two daughters and a son. Bates never remarried.

Bates was the nineteenth person to serve as principal of Tualatin Academy and, as it turned out, would be the last. Most of his predecessors had held the position for only one or two years, the exceptions being J. D. Robb and

D. L. Edwards, each of whom lasted for seven. "Prin Bates" stayed at his post for 22 years, working through the final period and last graduating class in 1915.

The closure of Tualatin Academy, mainly because of competition from the rising number of public high schools in the region, was a blow to the university in that it eliminated Pacific's primary "feeder" school. It also created a situation in which more and more students arrived as freshmen without any previous exposure to Congregational values. From Bates' perspective, this only increased the need to demonstrate those values by example as well as precept, a stance that contributed much to his immense popular-

Above: "Prin Bates" (left of the jump in white suit) at a pole-vaulting competition on campus
Below: The handbell used to summon students to class at the Tualatin Academy

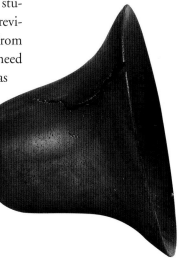

May Day Celebrations

$\mathcal{P}$ACIFIC UNIVERSITY staged its first May Day celebration just one month before the assassination of Archduke Ferdinand, which catapulted Europe into World War I. The idyllic all-day event, held May 16, 1914, included folk dances, singing, athletic competitions, plays, and a luncheon in Herrick Hall. Lura Tamiesie, a junior, was crowned "Queen of the May" and led a royal procession from Carnegie Library to the west side of Marsh Hall, amid students, faculty, and townspeople. The double-line procession included an assortment of colorful characters in Swedish, Japanese, Gypsy, and Native American costumes. Adding an odd touch of academia, Clinton Ostrander, the student body president, marched in his cap and gown. Flowers were everywhere and, according to the *Index,* "The may-pole which stood in the middle of the green was wound by girls in white with graceful steps and figures which made the winding beautiful and left the pole a slender column of pink and white." According to some estimates, the crowd that attended the evening pageant around the two bonfires on the campus was the largest ever to gather in Forest Grove.

The 1922 May Day followed an historical theme, depicting the "advance of religious education." The pageant included eighteenth-century colonials in silks and laces, pilgrims, knights wearing chain mail and helmets, Oregon Trail pioneers, American Indians, and fur trappers. In 1936, the event took a decidedly western turn when the men's ensemble sang "Home on the Range" and a group of 12 girls, dressed in cowboy suits, tap danced. By the 1950s, the event was indoors and called the May Day Coronation Ball. By this time, it resembled a typical formal dance.

May Day celebration on campus in 1951 (above) and 1914 (opposite)

From that successful beginning in 1914, May Day continued as one of Pacific's traditional "Festival Days" for over 50 years. Issues of the *Heart of Oak* yearbook contain stories and photos of May Day celebrations through the decades, highlighting the May Queen and the popular social pageantry of the day. This spring ritual slowed down and ended in the late 1960s, probably as a result of that decade's changing social attitudes. Karen Sato '66 was crowned May Queen in 1967, the last to be so honored.

ity among the students. As with McClelland and others, Bates' "liberal" views on education underscored and modernized the Congregational approach to ethics and civic responsibility, including a renewed emphasis on service to those less fortunate in other countries. Near the end of his career, Bates wrote: "The graduates of Pacific University number less than 400—its student body has never been large—but among that small number have been … the contributions of Pacific to the finest citizenship of the world at home and abroad."

Mary Frances Farnham (ca. 1913)

When Tualatin Academy closed, Bates became professor of philosophy at the university and dean of the faculty. In 1918, in recognition of his tireless work on behalf of Christian education, Bates received an honorary doctor of divinity degree from Pacific University. Upon retiring from his post at the university in 1926, he traveled to Greece and taught for a year in the American School of Religion in Athens. For the remainder of his life, Bates made his home in Forest Grove—for many years in an apartment over Paterson Furniture on Main Street—and maintained close ties with the university community. He died, at age 96, on October 23, 1949, Pacific's centennial year. In 1960 the former president's residence on campus, located on College Way, was officially named "Bates House" to acknowledge his steadfast and selfless contribution to the college.

"THE HANDIWORK OF A LOVELY SPIRIT"

Henry Bates' female counterpart as a principal and later as a dean was Mary Frances Farnham. As with the heads of the academy before Bates, most of the principals of the Ladies Department before Farnham had served only one to two years, the exceptions being the six-year terms of Luella Carson (1878–84) and Julia Adams (1885–91). Mary Farnham became principal in 1897 and remained in that posi-

tion for 18 years, after which she became dean of women at the university for another nine years. During her combined tenure in these positions, she saw five of Pacific University's 15 presidents come and go.

Mary Frances Farnham was born in 1847 in Bridgton, Maine, a small town that even today retains much of its rustic charm. After graduating from Mount Holyoke College in 1868, she returned to Bridgton to serve as superintendent of schools for three years. The next we hear of her she is in Capetown, South Africa, as vice principal of the Bloenhof School, a position she held for eight years until recurrent bouts of sunstroke got the better of her. She traveled extensively in Europe before returning to the States and taking on the position of preceptress at various schools, including Burr and Burton Seminary in Manchester, Vermont, Forest Park University in St. Louis, and again in Maine at Fryeburg Academy. Research work at Radcliffe in 1895–96 led to the publication of a documentary history of Maine by the Maine Historical Society. By the time she arrived at Pacific a year later she was a world traveler, experienced teacher, and published writer, by far the most prestigious faculty member ever to grace the "Ladies Department."

Farnham's tall, slim stature, stately mien, and trademark high-collared blue gown made her immediately recognizable even from a distance, and she seems to have been equally popular as an administrator and an instructor in English literature. Polly Hazzard Budrow, one of her former students, recalls that Miss Farnham made all of her classes, "even Shakespeare," lively and interesting through the use of an extensive collection of art reproductions on postcards, which are preserved in the Pacific University Museum. Mrs. Budrow, who was two days short of her 101st birthday when she spoke to the author, also recalls of Miss Farnham that "nothing could get her flustered," not even the ongoing attempts of the female students to romantically link her and "Prin Bates," a widower of two years when Farnham arrived at Pacific, on the grounds that they invariably sat at the same table in the dining hall.

Over the years, the *Heart of Oak* reads like a scrapbook of Mary Farnham's career at Pacific. The 1909 yearbook describes her as "a woman of the highest culture and refinement," adding that "the high social standard of our institution is due at least in a large measure to her influence." The 1913 annual notes that Miss Farnham was "especially famous as a 'Spring Lecturer' and ten o'clock extinguisher of Herrick Hall lights," adding as afterthought that "The Juniors can recommend Miss Farnham as a jolly chaperone." Her portraits convey, if not a jolly, at least a pleasant aspect, mingled with just enough hint of austerity to assure the errant student that she means business. The 1922 *Heart of Oak* is dedicated to Mary Farnham, who retired two years later.

Pacific University remained close to Mary Farnham's heart even after her retirement. She continued to take an active part in the Christmas Wassail, a long-standing tradition that she

A Trustee Goes Down with the Titanic

$\mathcal{A}$MONG THE LONG ODDS in Pacific University's long history are the chances of one of its trustees being on board R.M.S. Titanic during its maiden voyage in April 1912. But Frank Manley Warren, who had served on the Board of Trustees for nearly 17 years, was indeed a passenger on the famous steamship and, along with 1,500 others, died in the frigid waters of the north Atlantic. He and his wife, Anna—the daughter of founder Rev. George Atkinson—had been vacationing in Europe since the previous January, spending most of their time cruising the Mediterranean. Mrs. Warren survived the disaster.

A second-hand account of the Warrens' experience reads: "Among members of the Warren family, stories are still told of the chaos existing when the woefully inadequate lifeboats were launched, how Frank Warren embraced Mrs. Warren, bidding her

One of the lifeboats carrying RMS Titanic *survivors (women and children) photographed from the* Carpathia.

a last farewell, and then calmly stepped back on the listing deck as the women and children were lowered to the sea. In the darkness of the cold night, Mrs. Warren could not see her husband as she looked back, and he was not among the survivors brought to New York by the *Carpathia*."

Frank Warren, president of Warren Packing Company, had been a pioneer in the salmon canning industry on the Columbia River. In the early 1880s he began using giant fishwheels to efficiently catch thousands of salmon moving upriver. A cannery (in what is now Warrendale, which was named after him) was constructed to process the catch for market. The cannery ceased operation about 1930 and the federal government purchased the property to build Bonneville Dam.

The first gymnasium (left, top), which was formerly a Baptist Church, moved to the campus in the 1890s. It was replaced by a new gymnasium in 1910 (left).

Andrew Carnegie's Gift

*P*ACIFIC UNIVERSITY operated for over half a century—one-third of its existence—without a dedicated library structure on campus. Steel magnate Andrew Carnegie changed that when he provided a $20,000 gift to construct a building to house Pacific's collection of books, serials, and government documents. Carnegie's offer, made in April 1905, challenged the university to raise a matching amount for the continued maintenance of the library. Under those terms, it took another seven years before Carnegie Library opened its doors to grateful students and faculty.

Andrew Carnegie is well known for his philanthropy, especially his program of building over 1,600 public libraries in cities across the nation. The state of Oregon alone added 31 public libraries before World War I, using grants from Carnegie. Since the overall program had strict architectural guidelines, these distinctive buildings can be readily identified, regardless of their materials. Today many of these libraries, abandoned because of expanded collections and changing use patterns, have been converted into art centers and historical museums.

Pacific's new library, however, was part of a separate program established for "academic" libraries on college campuses. A total of 108 academic libraries were added nationwide. Surprisingly, Pacific University acquired the only one in the entire Pacific Northwest (the other two on the West Coast were constructed in California). Although speculative, it's probable that former president Thomas McClelland influenced the grant to Pacific. As a founding member of the Carnegie Foundation Board—and a personal friend of Andrew Carnegie—it seems likely that his continued interest in Pacific's welfare was a factor in the choice. Also noteworthy is the fact that Carnegie provided $10,000 toward the construction of the new Herrick Hall in 1907, only two years after his promise to fund the library project.

When the new Carnegie Library opened in the fall of 1912, the white brick structure—designed by the noted Portland architectural firm of Whidden and Lewis—was hailed as a symbolic milestone for the university. Unfortunately, it also initiated an era of hard times. President William Ferrin, strongly opposed to using inferior local building materials, resigned over the project. Ferrin, who followed Thomas McClelland as president, had joined the faculty in 1877. He was a native New Englander and served as a vital philosophical link to the Sidney Marsh era.

had begun while at Pacific, and she compiled an extensive profile of Pacific alumni.

In what may have been her last letter to President Walter Giersbach, in October of 1941, she apologizes that glaucoma and increasing infirmity prevent her from doing as much for the university as she would like to do: "I am simply expressing a wish that is uppermost—that I would gladly do more." She died a year later at the age of 96. At a memorial service in her honor, President Giersbach said of her: "There was hardly a matter touched by Mary Frances Farnham that did not show the handiwork of a lovely spirit, a mind as sharp as a copper etching."

FROM PROMISE TO PRESENTIMENT

With Henry Liberty Bates heading the Academy, Mary Farnham in charge of the Ladies Department, and President Ferrin carrying on the innovative work that Thomas McClelland had started at the college, the years 1900 to 1913 were marked by great progress and great promise. Campus expansion hit a temporary setback when Herrick Hall burned in 1906, but a new dormitory was in place by 1907, and in 1910 a new gymnasium was finished.

Even more impressive was the completion, in 1912, of the only academic library in the Northwest to be funded by Carnegie. By this time Pacific had shifted from a three-term schedule to a semester system; in 1913 it adopted majors and minors and even offered a nominal master's degree. In that same year it achieved accreditation from the U.S. Bureau of Education, a national feather in President Ferrin's cap.

The national craze for sports during these years (the first Rose Bowl game was held in 1902 and the first World Series in 1903) infected Pacific as well. In the fall, football fever (the "rugby" had been dropped and helmets had been added) ran high; in the spring, the baseball team took to the field, and the track team, inspired by Tualatin Academy alumnus A. C. Gilbert's winning a gold medal in the 1908 Olympic Games in London, gave its all

for the P. U. Crimson and Black. In 1904, led by Gilbert in his last spring on campus, Pacific had won the State track championship, an impressive feat for a college of its size. Debating, too, was still considered a major sport, and in 1909 when Pacific defeated both Willamette and Whitman Colleges in debate, the students cheered the contests and lit great bonfires to celebrate the victory. The winter season ushered in student minstrel shows, singnights, and, under the watchful eye of Mary Farnham, the Christmas Wassail. As always, music was a big part of campus life, with faculty members giving regular recitals for the townspeople of Forest Grove. On every front, Pacific was a vital force in the community and seemed on track to becoming one of the preeminent small colleges on the West Coast.

Even before the closure of the Tualatin Academy, however, Pacific's fortunes had taken a turn for the worse. President Ferrin, never popular with the trustees, had a major falling out with the Board over the use of inferior local material for the new library and the school's failure to match an offer of $100,000 from railroad tycoon James Jerome Hill of St. Paul, Minn. Moreover, Ferrin's administrative style had been a sore point with the faculty from the beginning. On June 29, 1912, the faculty finally tendered a petition, signed by both Bates and Farnham among others, calling the president "a task master in the art of caustic speech" and demanding his resignation.

In 1913, at a point when Pacific's future should have looked brightest, William Ferrin resigned after 36 years of association with the college. It would prove a turning point in the school's history. In the decade that followed, Pacific University would go through three presidents, a series of failed fund-raising attempts, and rumors of imminent closure that were, alas, well-founded.

An able professor but a beleaguered president, William Ferrin (ca. 1880) ultimately resigned under pressure from the faculty. After itemizing the damage done on several fronts by Ferrin's "lack of tact" and "arbitrary manner," the faculty petition added, in a lighter vein: "It has been said by some that the fire of his tongue and the color of his hair caused the burning of the Congregational Church some years ago."

Pacific University band (ca. 1910)

"Trying Times": The Lean Years and John Dobbs

During these trying times … the college has gone quietly on its way holding up the most excellent in all things.

—JOHN FRANCIS DOBBS,
in a letter to Mary Frances Farnham, April 1, 1937

John Dobbs

ERE THE 150-YEAR HISTORY of Pacific University represented by a vital signs monitor, the years 1914–1924 would show up on the screen as an alarmingly flat line accompanied by a prolonged warning beep. This is not to suggest that the campus was unlively during the "Roaring Twenties." Dancing at last became permissible during this period and vigorous "Boxer tosses" would become the stuff of legend for future alumni. Also, the name "Badgers" was adopted by Pacific's athletic teams in 1921 after someone at a football game shouted that the Crimson and Black were "fighting like Badgers!" But from an institutional point of view, the college was on hold during this decade and, despite an administrative upturn in 1925 in the person of President John Dobbs, would remain in survival mode through World War II.

THE DEPRESSION BEFORE THE DEPRESSION

As early as 1915 a note of suppressed alarm appears in the pages of Pacific University's school newspaper, the *Index*. Under the enthusiastic headline "The Phenomenal Growth of the College," an editorial notes that the enrollment at the college has grown to 215, adding, "If this increase is maintained, we shall have at least 300 or 400 students … within the next four or five years."

This optimistic prediction, however, is immediately qualified: "The large problem of the immediate future is the expansion of the endowment to meet the inevitable growth of the College." Most telling, perhaps, is the sentence that immediately follows: "Pacific University is certainly not a decadent institution, but one of large vitality, vigor and service for this part of the country." That the *Index* feels compelled to deny that the college is "decadent," and to insert the qualifier "for this part of the country," is a far cry from the confident exuberance

Five victorious sophomores (ca. 1927) pose with a Boxer that is showing the ravages of being "tossed."

Charles Bushnell

Robert Fry Clark

William Weir

that prevailed in its pages during and immediately following the McClelland decade.

The sense of foreboding was not unjustified. In the next 10 years, the enrollment of the college would see a net gain of three students—hardly "phenomenal growth." (By way of comparison, Whitman College, which had been founded later than Pacific and by one of Pacific's former faculty, grew from 176 students in 1906 to an enrollment of 608 in 1926.) Enlistment for service in World War I accounted for the lack of students during part of this period; the school opened in 1918 with only two male students—one who had been rejected by the draft board and one who was Japanese. But there were other reasons as well. Ironically, the same improved roads that had brought metropolitan culture to Forest Grove were now taking prospective local students to

Portland and elsewhere, reflecting a national trend that saw 1920 as the first year when the U.S. population was more urban than rural.

By 1916, the trustees could see the writing on the wall and were beginning to panic. In a creative—some would say "desperate"—attempt to turn things around, President Ferrin's successor, Charles Bushnell, pushed for a merger with the smaller Albany College, a Presbyterian institution some 50 miles to the south. The proposed merger captured the interest and energies of many, but old rivalries between the Congregationalists and the Presbyterians surfaced, and neither school had the leadership to get beyond the discussion stage.

In 1918 President Bushnell resigned, largely out of frustration over the stalled merger. He was succeeded by Robert Fry Clark, who, with degrees from Oberlin and Chicago, seemed like

Mrs. McCormick: A Tale of Two Buildings

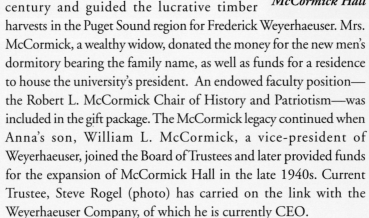

Anna McCormick

Although President Weir's administration lasted only two years, he should be credited with raising funds for two new buildings on campus—McCormick Hall and the President's House (now Bates House). Prior to leaving Bellingham, Washington, Weir cemented a strong relationship with Anna McCormick of Tacoma. Anna's deceased husband, Robert L. McCormick, relocated at the turn-of-the-century and guided the lucrative timber harvests in the Puget Sound region for Frederick Weyerhaeuser. Mrs. McCormick, a wealthy widow, donated the money for the new men's dormitory bearing the family name, as well as funds for a residence to house the university's president. An endowed faculty position— the Robert L. McCormick Chair of History and Patriotism—was included in the gift package. The McCormick legacy continued when Anna's son, William L. McCormick, a vice-president of Weyerhaeuser, joined the Board of Trustees and later provided funds for the expansion of McCormick Hall in the late 1940s. Current Trustee, Steve Rogel (photo) has carried on the link with the Weyerhaeuser Company, of which he is currently CEO.

McCormick Hall

Steven Rogel

Top: Pacific's 1914 entry in the Portland Rose Festival Parade illustrates the "progress of higher education in Oregon." Above: The 1921 Northwest Champions football team—Coach Leo Frank (top row, far right) was responsible for the name "Badgers."

both an educational leader and a builder. When the war ended, the return of ex-servicemen bolstered enrollment, but, since the college granted them free tuition, it did little to help the financial crisis. In 1920 Clark, noting that "Unless aid comes speedily and in considerable amount the institution will be compelled to close," announced a $2 million fund drive for an endowment and six new buildings. Within two years, however, the fund drive had lapsed and Clark announced the need to find $25,000 just to keep the school afloat. In the face of imminent closure and a vote of no-confidence from trustees and alumni alike, Clark too was forced to resign.

The trustees then appointed William Weir, a geologist and veteran fund-raiser from Bellingham Normal School, who resurrected the negotiations for a merger with Albany College. When it became clear, however, that

joining forces with Albany entailed the prospect of a Presbyterian take-over of Pacific, Weir abandoned the idea. Six years of on-again off-again negotiations had come to nothing, President Weir resigned after only two years at the helm, and morale at Pacific was at an all-time low. Albany College, incidentally, would later move to Portland and, in 1942, would become Lewis and Clark College.

THE LAST CONGREGATIONALIST: JOHN DOBBS

When Rev. John Francis Dobbs entered the scene as Pacific's president in 1925, he found a university with shrinking prospects and escalating financial worries. Undaunted, President

Campus "clean up" day was a fall tradition.
Top: In the 1920s President Robert Fry Clark, second from left, and Henry Liberty Bates (in overalls and a tie) join students and staff.
Above: During "Clean up Day" in 1917 the students and faculty took the opportunity to have fun dressing the part.

Mr. Gilbert's Toys

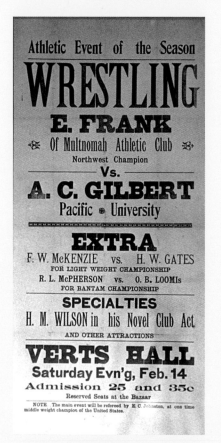

Above: a 1903 poster announcing the "Athletic Event of the Season." The rematch between Edgar Frank and A. C. Gilbert took place in Verts Hall, a once-popular gathering place in Forest Grove.

PERHAPS the most nationally famous individual to come out of Tualatin Academy and Pacific University was Alfred Carlton Gilbert (1884–1961). Driven by an intensely competitive nature, A. C. Gilbert actively pursued a multitude of passions throughout his life—magic, athletics, big game hunting, and especially educational toys for children. He is best known for his innovative construction toy—Erector—started in 1913 and manufactured by the Gilbert Toy Company for the next 50 years. Countless children used Erector sets to assemble realistic aircraft, ferris wheels, carousels, lift cranes, vehicles, and other toys. Nationwide, the Erector set—sold in its trademark red-metal box—is embedded in our popular culture.

A. C. Gilbert was born in Salem, Oregon, and raised in a Congregationalist atmosphere. His paternal uncle, Andrew T. Gilbert, joined Pacific University's Board of Trustees in 1896, so it was no surprise when Alfred, along with his older brother Harold, later enrolled in Tualatin Academy. Always a sports enthusiast, A. C. gained statewide fame for his feats of strength and leadership in track-and-field, wrestling, and football. He held the official world's record for pull-ups while a student in Tualatin Academy and was later called by the *Oregonian* newspaper "the best quarterback to be found in Oregon." He graduated from Tualatin Academy in 1902, then matriculated into Pacific University. In 1904 he led the P.U. track team to a state championship, putting the crimson and black into the limelight. After two years at Pacific, Gilbert transferred to Yale University to pursue a medical degree (he thought it would make him a better coach). The highlight of his athletic career came in 1908 when he won a gold medal in the pole vault at the Olympic Games in London.

Erector was not Gilbert's only product. He is credited with developing the S-gauge model train after purchasing the American Flyer company in the 1930s, turning that brand into the most realistic on the market. Gilbert's engineers also solved the problem of designing small electric motors by inventing enameled wire, making it possible to power not only the toys he sold but his company's household appliances as well (Gilbert is

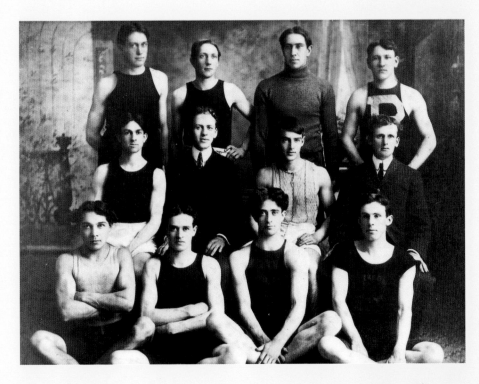

Future Olympic gold medalist A.C. Gilbert (middle row, second from right) and the 1904 track team

responsible for one of the first portable fans). Many people today clearly recall their Gilbert Chemistry Sets, common in the 1950s, and other educational sets. The Gilbert Toy Company even marketed an Atomic Energy Set, but this was quickly pulled from the market because of the radioactive material in the kit. The toy empire he started in 1913 eventually made him a millionaire, and he spent the remaining years of his life in Connecticut on a large estate he called "Paradise."

Gilbert's 1954 autobiography, *The Man Who Lives in Paradise*, makes it clear that his energy while in Forest Grove was not focused exclusively on academic pursuits. His forte, when not on the athletic field, was engaging in campus pranks: putting chickens in upright pianos, removing the bell from Science Hall (now Old College Hall), and attempting to hoist a donkey into Marsh Hall's Brighton Chapel—through the second-floor window. These and other high-jinks endeared him to many of his classmates, one of whom—Mary Thompson—became his future bride. They were married in September, 1908.

Below: Erector Set made by the Gilbert Toy Company in the 1950s

Dobbs assessed the problems and set about to find creative solutions. Then, four years after he started, the Great Depression hit and brought the university once again to the brink of closure. That Pacific University survived the Depression era at all, given its weakened state at the outset, is amazing; that it emerged from the end of that dark tunnel with a $300,000 endowment and the elimination of a $40,000 debt is a lasting credit to the work of John Francis Dobbs.

Like many of his predecessors, Rev. John Dobbs was a New Englander—a "rock-ribbed, starched-collared New Englander," as one alumnus remembers him. He came to Forest Grove from Malden, Massachusetts, where he had filled the pulpit of the Congregational church. He had studied at Lafayette and Union Theological Seminaries but, unlike most of his predecessors, had virtually no background in education. His inexperience in academic politics would prove a weakness in the long run, but it allowed him initially to apply an outsider's fresh outlook to the university's woes.

Dobbs had his work cut out for him. He began by instituting a three-year plan that called for a 50 percent raise in tuition to $150 per year, an increase in the student body to 250, and a new science building. At the end of 1926, he launched a $350,000 endowment campaign in Portland, aimed at Congregational constituents. Although Dobbs never saw a new science building, he did stem the damaging attrition at Pacific, which regularly saw a student body with nearly half freshmen and only a handful of seniors.

Unfortunately, the financial doldrums that came on the heels of the 1929 Crash made it impossible for Dobbs and the Board of Trustees to do anything beyond scrambling to survive. But school spirits had been raised, at least temporarily, and President Dobbs continued to earn the respect, if not always the affection, of faculty and students through his example and his talks, which often dealt with issues of service to humankind and the search for truth.

Carolyn Dobbs, the president's wife, was also active on campus, developing a keen interest in Oregon history. She researched the famous 1843 vote to form a civil government in Oregon, and in 1932 authored a popular book, *Men of Champoeg*, based on her investigations. Reversing the trend of spending protracted time away from the institution, John and Carolyn Dobbs lived on campus with their two children, in the president's residence, and interacted daily with the learning community. Every morning, rain or shine, President Dobbs could be seen going down the sidewalk and turning the corner to the long walkway leading to the main entrance of Marsh Hall.

Dobbs' effectiveness began to wane, however, in the pre-war years. His repeated references to Pacific as the "little old New England College of the West" began to grate on students' ears, and what some considered his puritanical ethos ran counter to the emancipating influence of the Silver Screen and the Big Band Era in the years immediately preceding World War II. By 1939, many students considered Dobbs an anachronism—this in a year when two of the films nominated for best picture were "Gone with the Wind" and "Goodbye Mr. Chips." Like Scarlett O'Hara and Mr. Chips, President Dobbs' greatest strength and greatest weakness may well have been that he did not bend with the times.

QUALITY VERSUS QUANTITY

Whatever his faults, John Dobbs was nothing if not consistent. Throughout his tenure at Pacific, he stressed the importance of Christian values and a liberal arts education as the foundation for a broader understanding of the world. Historian James Hitchman, writing in 1981, notes:

"Scores of other small college presidents were saying the same thing at the time and had been saying it for a century and more, but the point is that Dobbs is an example of inculcating a moral dimension into student outlook characteristic of the church-related liberal arts college

William G. Hale, '03, went on to earn a Harvard law degree, and to distinguish himself as dean of the law schools at the Universities of Oregon, Southern California, and Illinois.

The Hawaiian Connection

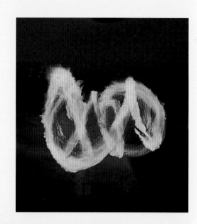

O N   H I S   V O Y A G E   T O   O R E G O N in 1848, Rev. George Atkinson spent several weeks in the Sandwich Islands, as Hawaii was known at the time. His journal describes the beauty of the tropical vegetation and the volcanic formations. When he later worked to establish Pacific University, the thought of Hawaiians attending the school probably never crossed his mind.

When Hawaii became the 50th state on August 21, 1959, however, Pacific University immediately started cultivating a close relationship with its residents. President Miller Ritchie's arrival on campus at the same time served as the catalyst for increased recruitment of Hawaiian students. His inauguration on March 6, 1960 included a powerful symbol of this new connection: Hawaii's first governor, William F. Quinn received an honorary Doctor of Laws degree. Oregon's own governor, Mark O. Hatfield, also attended the ceremony, held in the high school gymnasium because Pacific had no indoor facility large enough for the crowd. (This too would change during the Miller Ritchie administration.)

During the 1959–60 academic year, students formed the Hawaiian Club (Nā Haumāna O Hawai'i) on campus "to display the Hawaiian spirit in their service to the school and community." Dr. Fred Scheller '61 served as the faculty advisor, and Tagay Kang was elected president of the club. The Hawaiian Club started the annual luau during this time, a much-loved tradition that has grown into a major extravaganza every spring. Pacific still recruits heavily in the Hawaiian Islands, and the Hawaiian Club remains one of the most active on campus.

Top and middle: The popular "Fire Dance" is a staple of today's Luau celebrations, here performed by Brock Whittington '95.

Right: An early Luau held on the lawns behind Bates House on College Way (ca. 1960)

*Top: archery
in the 1940s
Right: Pacific marked its
centennial year in 1949 —
Herrick Hall is in the
background.*

SPLENDID AUDACITY: THE STORY OF PACIFIC UNIVERSITY

that put a different stamp upon its undergraduates than those of state or larger institutions."

As Hitchman's summation suggests, the secret to Dobbs' relative success during his 16-year term as president of Pacific was his clear sense of the school's identity as a "small … church-related liberal arts college." How accurate this was in fact is a different question.

That Pacific was small was incontestable. That it was "church-related" would take on a different meaning with Dobbs' departure in 1940, for he was the last of Pacific's presidents who was also a Congregationalist minister. And while Dobbs consistently stressed traditional "liberal arts" values, the truth is that Pacific was more of a "normal school," preparing most of its graduates for careers as teachers. Finally, as to whether Pacific was a "college" or, as Sidney Harper Marsh had insisted, a "university," the nominal issue remained a source of embarrassment to some. As Henry Liberty Bates had once asserted, "The name 'University' has always been somewhat of a misnomer. It reflects the high aims and worthy aspirations of its early founders rather than actual achievements in the shape of graduate courses and professional schools."

But in Dobbs' mind at least, the university—or whatever one chose to call it—was doing what it was meant to do, turning disadvantaged, rural youth into solid citizens with sound moral values. As he put it in a letter preserved in the University Archives: "Out of 'the sticks' … come many of the finest young people at Pacific. They are clean, strong, and industrious, and deserve their chance at higher education."

In fact, despite Pacific's lagging enrollment during the first four decades of the twentieth century, many of its alumni went on to prominent careers. In 1919 five members of the Oregon State Legislature were Pacific alumni. A notable graduate of 1912 was Olaus J. Murie, who went on to an illustrious career as a biologist, nature artist, and conservationist. A 1915 graduate, Harvey Inlow, became president of what is now Eastern Oregon State University. Another graduate, William G. Hale, went on to earn a Harvard law degree and to distinguish himself as dean of the law schools at the Universities of Oregon, Southern California, and Illinois. Thomas S. Thompson and Leland Johnson, both graduates of 1938, went on to become the presidents of, respectively, Morningside College and the First National Bank of Oregon. On the literary home front, the work of Verne Bright, '25, appeared in well over 100 different publications, earning him a national, if ephemeral, reputation as a poet. And, of course, former track star A. C. Gilbert brought joy to several generations of American children with his invention of the Erector set.

But numbers did matter, even to Dobbs, who proudly pointed out to former Dean of Women Mary Farnham in 1937 that "Our freshman class was 147 this year, much the largest in the history of the college." And while enrollment at Pacific reached an all-time high of 348 in Dobbs' last year as president, it would, within three years of his departure, drop to around 150, well below what it had been in 1915 when the *Index* had predicted "phenomenal growth."

The major reason for this decline, of course, was loss of male students to World War II. Whatever the reasons, however, the bottom line was that the Pacific University of 1945 bore an embarrassing resemblance to the Pacific University of 1915. With a shoestring enrollment and the university faculty earning salaries well below those of Portland high school teachers, Pacific limped through the war years, waiting for the return of students and of that less tangible commodity, hope.

Marsh Hall wears a mantle of ivy in this photograph taken in 1944.

An Eye to the Future:
The College of Optometry

This was the beginning of the end of this young profession's inferiority feelings about itself and its professional education. — HAROLD M. HAYNES, O.D.

*I*T WOULD BE EASY to attribute Pacific's recurrent woes during the years 1914–1944 to inadequate endowment and lack of financial support. But while problems of funding were real and relentless enough, the institutional lethargy during this period had deeper roots. The truth is that Pacific University was the victim of a prolonged identity crisis. Was it a university in fact or only in name? In either case, to what degree was it Congregationalist? Was it small by default or, as Henry Liberty Bates had declared, by design? Should it adapt to "modern" values and ideas or resist them as secular and decadent? Sidney Harper Marsh had early pointed out the "defect in organization" in the school; by 1944 there seemed to be not so much a defect in organization as a defect in vision. The unforeseen solution that presented itself, therefore, was both symbolic and fitting: a college of optometry.

Below: an original Chamber's-Inskeep ophthalmometer (invented ca. 1870)

"A SAFE HAVEN"

Mary Frances Farnham (see p. 72) spent the last 13 years of her life in the Mann Home, located on 31st and NE Sandy Boulevard in Portland. It was from this location, now an Eastern meditation center and ashram, that at age 95 she wrote to Pacific president Walter Giersbach apologizing that glaucoma prevented her from doing more than she would like to have done for the university.

Just blocks away, on 41st and NE Sandy, was the North Pacific College of Optometry, which housed a small clinic. Given the proximity, it is altogether possible that Pacific's former dean of women visited that neighborhood optometry clinic to have her vision tested. In any case, the conjecture is a pleasing one, since it was to the North Pacific College of Optometry that, three years after Farnham's death, her beloved university would also turn to get its future more clearly in focus.

Like Forest Grove in the 1840s, Portland's Sandy Boulevard in the 1940s was not a likely place for a college of any kind, and the North Pacific College of Optometry hardly looked the part. The spot was, and is, dominated by the old Hollywood Theater, one of the last vaudeville-house movie palaces built in Portland, which had opened in 1926 to the accompaniment of a $40,000 Wurlitzer organ and an eight-piece orchestra. A magnet for development in what is now the "Hollywood District," the only area in Portland named after a local building, the theater attracted a motley assortment of small

Top: Classroom in the basement of Marsh Hall (ca. 1950) and (above) a class in Jefferson Hall

businesses, a boon for the optometry college and clinic.

Dr. Clarence "Clary" Carkner, who has been called "the Father of the College of Optometry at Pacific University," recalls that when he came from Saskatchewan, Canada to study at North Pacific College of Optometry he was shocked to find that the "campus" consisted of about 400 square feet in the second story of an old brick building attached by a walkway to a movie theater. Dr. Newton Wesley, who had become an optometrist because his mother wanted him to be a doctor and he "didn't like blood," recalls that to get to the second floor you had to go through the Hollywood Arcade, with its magazine and tobacco shops (the arcade, along with the original site of the optometry college, burned to the ground in 1997). Both agree, however, that the training in optometry was excellent at North Pacific, which had been founded in 1919 when the DeKeyser Institute of Optometry merged with the Oregon College of Ocular Sciences.

Optometry in the 1940s was not the respected profession it is today. Many optometrists operated out of jewelry stores. The "real" schools of medicine, conveniently forgetting that surgery had its origins in barber shops, sought to distance themselves from colleges of optometry, all of which were independent and proprietary in any case. Columbia University

had established the first university-sponsored course in optometry in 1910, but this was in the Department of Extension Education, and without the approval of the medical school. By 1930 Columbia was giving a four-year course in optometry for a B.Sc. degree, but no university gave a doctoral degree in optometrics. In 1934 the American Medical Association (AMA) resolved to stop optometrists from prescribing glasses in hospitals, and in 1935 declared it unethical for any AMA member to teach or consult with an optometrist.

Shortly later, Columbia University dropped its courses in optometry, setting a precedent that threatened to make it even more difficult for independent colleges of optometry—even the good ones—to receive academic accreditation of any kind. Dr. Wesley recalls a visitor to North Pacific College of Optometry who came offering accreditation in exchange for $3,000 under the table. According to Wesley, two students—there were only about 50 students at the college at the time—threw the intruder down the stairs.

It was in such a climate that, in 1945, the principals of the North Pacific College of Optometry, which had suspended operation in 1943 because of the war, decided they would have to align their fortunes with an academic institution if their degree of doctor of optometry was going to have any meaning. They had earlier gone through preliminary negotiations with Lewis and Clark College, but these had come to naught—an interesting gloss on Pacific University's history of failed mergers with that institution when it was still Albany College. Now, given the open hostility of the AMA, they were wary of schools with a strong premed component and were looking instead for a liberal arts college to lend academic standing to their course of training. As Dr. Wesley put it, they wanted a "safe haven" from what amounted to outright persecution by the medical profession.

JOINING FORCES

Meanwhile, back at Pacific University, President Walter Giersbach and the trustees were

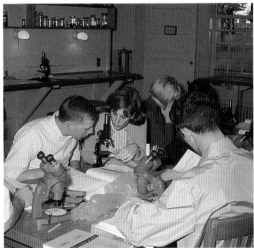

Left: Jefferson Hall was built in 1952 to house the flourishing College of Optometry; the building was expanded in 1967 (Brombach wing on the east side) and again in 1999.

Right: An optometry class in Jefferson Hall in 1967

beginning to realize that adopting some special, professional program beyond the liberal arts offerings would go far toward providing extra funds and attracting a cadre of new undergraduates. Such a move would also lend credibility to the name "university" and, in the bargain, would offer a needed professional service to the region. This was not an uncommon strategy for small colleges in the Northwest at the time, and would eventually become standard practice: the University of Puget Sound would become known for occupational therapy, Linfield College for its research institute, Pacific Lutheran for business, Willamette and Whitman Colleges for pre-med, Lewis and Clark for law, and Whitworth for nursing.

None of the parties involved seems to recall who approached whom first, but once broached, the idea of establishing a college of optometry at Pacific University met little resistance. Several meetings of both parties were held in downtown Portland, and hard questions about academic and professional standards were asked and resolved. Dr. Wesley, who, along with Dr. Roy Clunes, was co-owner of the North Pacific College of Optometry, was involved in these negotiations only in absentia; being of Japanese ancestry, he and his family spent the war years in an internment camp in Oregon. He later went on to do pioneering work in the development of contact lenses.

In August of 1945, the *Oregonian* announced the outcome of the several meetings:

Fire Destroys Original College of Optometry Building

Portland, OR—March 6, 1997: Firemen work for hours in an attempt to save the original site of North Pacific College of Optometry, on 41st and NE Sandy Boulevard. In 1945, North Pacific merged with Pacific University and moved its facilities from the second story of the above building to the campus in Forest Grove. Despite firemen's efforts, the old quarters of North Pacific College of Optometry burned to the ground, but the historic Hollywood Theater, which had been connected to the college by a second-floor walkway, was saved.

Jefferson Hall, which underwent a $3.5 million renovation in 1998-99, was rededicated in October, 1999.

North Pacific College of Optometry, the only school of optometry in the Northwest, became a part of Pacific University in Forest Grove, Oregon, Tuesday with a transfer of the college's corporate charter at a luncheon at the Benson Hotel … Official presentation of the charter to Dr. W. C. Giersbach, President of Pacific, was made by Dr. Frank Bemis, president of the Oregon Optometric Association.

The new college of optometry operated at first in the basement of Marsh Hall, which had only recently been emptied of its cords of slab wood when the college switched to oil heating. As Dr. Richard Feinberg, appointed dean of the college in 1948, recalled in 1970, "Every foot of space had to be fought for." Nor was space the only source of friction. Dr. Carol Pratt, one of Feinberg's predecessors, noted:

The earlier deans of the College of Optometry of Pacific University had rough experiences. The first dean lasted twenty-five hours, unable to contribute much to

the operation. The second dean lasted about a year before an approach to a nervous breakdown, exacerbated by difficulties with the administration, terminated his services. I served next in this tenuous position and lasted for a year also.

Despite the cramped quarters and the near nervous breakdowns, the new optometry school flourished, and in the spring of 1952 would move to a new home in Jefferson Hall.

In a joint effort with the Oregon Optometric Association, Pacific University developed a program leading to an academic doctor of optometry degree, the first ever recognized by the National Association for Accreditation of Colleges. Dr. Harold Haynes, who would serve as professor of optometry at Pacific for nearly 50 years, recalled the reaction that he and his classmates at Northern Illinois College had on hearing the news:

I can remember the excitement that was ours when we read in the Optometric Weekly that Pacific University was founding a college which would grant the O.D. degree and set a precedent that all other university schools were to follow years later.

Apparently, three O.D. degrees were conferred in 1947 and six in 1948, though as late as 1970, in a retrospective issue of *The Oregon Optometrist*, the alumni of these respective classes were still engaged in some good-natured wrangling over who received their degrees first. Clarence Bondelid, then at the University of Washington, noted:

> While some of the records show that the first graduating class received the O.D. degree in 1948, I have a diploma which reads August 13, 1947, and which grants me the O.D. degree. ... Fall[ing] back on a surname which starts with B ... I lay claim to being the first graduate in that first class of three, the other two being Cliff Haser and Don Gottlieb.

Whoever was first, the North Pacific College of Optometry had found its safe haven, and Pacific University, having established the first of its health profession programs, would never again have to apologize for calling itself a "university."

With veterans returning in large numbers and a bona fide professional college in place, Pacific University began to thrive—at least in terms of enrollment. Within three years of the war's end, the student body soared to an unprecedented high of 925 undergraduate students, more than half of its present size. To accommodate the influx of students, President Giersbach secured two wooden structures from Camp Adair—an infantry training camp near Corvallis, Oregon—and bricked them over to serve as a science building (named "Warner

Hall" after former trustee and benefactor Franklin Warner) and a campus bookstore and student union facility (named "Tabitha Brown Hall"). He also brought 10 barracks from Vancouver, Washington, to serve as housing for veterans and their families. One of these temporary buildings, incidentally, was christened "Farnham Hall," the university's first and last gesture toward preserving the memory of its longest-serving dean of women.

There would be further "trying times" for Pacific University, including President Giersbach's forced resignation in 1953. But beginning in 1945 the vital signs monitor began to show a strong and steady heartbeat. The patient was going to live.

Top: An aerial photograph from the 1950s (taken from the southeast) clearly shows Warner and Tabitha Brown Halls (moved from Camp Adair in Corvallis) on the south side of campus, as well as 10 barrack buildings on the east side. Bottom: World War II took students away from Pacific to serve in the armed forces. First Lieutenant Arthur C. Dixon, Jr. receives the Bronze Star in June 1945.

ACT III

Keeping the Vision Alive

1946-1999

An Era of Expansion: The Post-War Years and Miller Ritchie

The promised land is always a far distance. — MILLER RITCHIE

THE YEARS immediately following World War II were kind to Pacific University, if granting a reprieve from pummeling can be considered an act of kindness. In 1948 the college still operated with a deficit of $83,000 dollars and still carried a debt of some $20,000; but enrollment, along with school spirit, was high. The college offered 21 majors, with journalism being the most popular, and physical education, business, and sociology leading the rest of the pack. Throughout the Eisenhower era, Pacific could pass muster with its rival small colleges in the Northwest on all fronts. All, that is, except the condition of its physical plant, which had not seen any significant improvement in many years. The motto of Pacific was still "For Christ and His Kingdom," but it might well have been "What you don't see is what you get." The 1960s, and the leadership of President Miller Ritchie, would change all that.

AN INJECTION OF WORLDLINESS

The mood on college campuses in the postwar years reflected the mood of the country—optimistic, edging toward carefree. Alumni from the '40s are almost universally positive about the influence of their years at Pacific, and several of them went on to distinguished careers—Dr. Roy Lieuallen as one of Oregon's most effective and respected chancellors of higher education, Donald Bryant as director of Oregon's Educational and Public Broadcasting Service, Clinton Gruber as director of the Oregon Museum of Science and Industry, and Marjorie Moon as Idaho State Treasurer.

The presence of ex-servicemen, some of them with families, tended to loosen things up on campus. For example, the non-smoking policy remained on the books, but getting the former GIs to observe it was another matter. It was during this period too that a Pi Delta Epsilon wag named Douglas Culbertson launched the Northwest's "first all-college humor magazine," called "The P.U. Stinker"—a less than respectful play on Pacific's "time-honored *nomina duogrammata*"—which featured buxom "pin-ups" and off-color puns. The magazine ran from 1948 through 1954 before it petered out, as the "Stinker" might have put it.

Pacific's success in athletics—especially football—also served to bolster school spirit. The "Badgers" became a force to be reckoned with in the Northwest Conference. Football coach Paul Stagg, son of Notre Dame's famous Amos

Dr. Roy Lieuallen '40, chancellor of higher education in Oregon, 1961–1982

Greek Letter Societies

The Alpha Zetas present President Nixon with Boxer (temporarily) in 1968.

Below: The Fall 1956 Gamma Sigma Pledge Class

RATERNITIES AND SORORITIES have long been a part of college life on American campuses, though their function, popularity, and public image have changed dramatically over the past 150 years.

Pacific University gained its first fraternity early in its history when the Gamma Sigma society was granted a charter in 1863. Eight years later, in 1871, the women on campus organized the Philomathean society. (This sorority changed its name in 1924 to Phi Lambda Omicron, but they are still commonly known as the "Philos.")

As elsewhere, the original Greek letter groups at Pacific were called "literary societies." The 1870 catalog described them as "an approved method of supplementing the instruction of Teachers," and "an important instrument of education." In those days, the faculty granted charters to the Greek societies, which were expected to "subserve the general purpose of the institution." Activities, all academic in nature, included debates, public speaking, and music.

As interest in literary societies grew at the turn-of-the-century, two new groups splintered off from the old established ones: Alpha Zeta in 1901 (from the Gamma Sigmas) and Kappa Delta in 1904 (from the Philomatheans). This trend continued gradually for the next several years. As fraternities and sororities multiplied, their primary purpose shifted away from strict academic pursuits toward social activities, especially between the fraternities and sororities. In 1925 the Phi Alpha Tau society was Pacific's first, and only, national honor fraternity.

In 1928 the Gamma Sigma society became the first to acquire its own house off campus. The Alpha Zetas followed suit in 1932. These houses, however, were relatively short-lived experiments. Off-campus housing was again attempted by both fraternities in the late 1940s. (Only one fraternity, the Phi Beta Tau, has ever obtained a house with historic ties to Pacific; in the 1960s, they bought the former residence of Alanson Hinman on Hawthorne Street.)

*A Pajama Dance held by Theta Nu Alpha at the
Forest Grove Country Club in February, 1955*

Following a decline in interest during the Depression and WW II, the decades of the 1950s and 1960s saw a dramatic increase in the number of Greeks on campus, including several chapters of national societies. By 1958 Pacific boasted 12 different fraternities and sororities, though their activities by this time were a far cry from the early "literary societies." The high point came in the early 1970s when the number soared to 16, a rather ambitious level for a small college. Social changes during the next 20 years—including negative attitudes about fraternities and sororities—had an adverse impact on recruitment. The number of active Greek letter societies dwindled, and over the past decade the total has hovered between four and six.

Perhaps not surprisingly, the four oldest and most established organizations have evolved and survived. In fact, the Gamma Sigma society is among the oldest local fraternities in the western United States. Fraternities and sororities at Pacific, besides being the source of much nostalgia and many colorful stories at class reunions, continue to give students some grounding in the tradition of community service and fellowship.

*A "boxer toss," such as this one in the
late '40s (Boxer is presumed to be
under the cloud of dust left of the
center of the photograph), was often a
contest between Greek societies.*

Walter Giersbach

Alonzo Stagg, recruited a string of players from New Jersey that included halfback Frank Buckiewicz, who would become a Little All-American and later a long-time coach at Pacific. Students thronged to the games, and the *Index* weekly touted the gridiron prowess of the Crimson and Black—a far cry from the day in 1892 when only three or four students had any knowledge of Pacific's first football game.

Sororities and fraternities expanded during these years as well, adding to the general *joie de vivre*. In the early '50s, fraternity high jinks that would have appalled former President Dobbs became the order of the day, including the inevitable "panty-raids" and Gamma Sigma initiation rites such as "kidnapping" sorority members, and leaving them tied to chairs in various public locations. Testosterone, grease, and chrome were plentiful in the pre-Elvis years. In the freshman class of 1953 men outnumbered women two to one, while the sophomore ratio was nearly four to one, the juniors three to one, and the seniors slightly more than two to one. Of the 132 students enrolled in the College of Optometry, only one was female.

Despite the injection of worldliness, most students continued to profess some church affiliation. Interestingly, however, of the 553 stu-

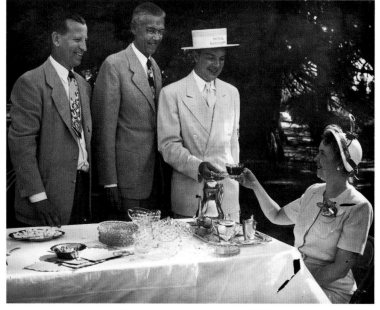

Marion Giersbach serves tea in the president's garden following a dedication ceremony for a rose garden in June 1949.

dents enrolled in 1953, Methodists heavily outnumbered the Congregationalists (95 to 55), with Catholics (48) coming in a close third. Also represented were Lutherans, Baptists, Presbyterians, Latter Day Saints, Jews, Christian Scientists, Seventh Day Adventists, Episcopalians, Evangelicals, Anglicans, Buddhists, Mennonites, and one Orthodox Syrian. Clearly, the once-heated question of whether Pacific was a Congregationalist college had become something of a moot point.

IMPORTANT ADVANCES

Throughout these years, President Giersbach was seldom on campus, though his wife, Marion, hosted innumerable teas and, in addition to her duties as the mother of three boys, also served as surrogate mother to the outnumbered female students, many of whom remember her with special fondness. Marion Giersbach also became the first curator of the Pacific University Museum in 1949, and would later write a history of Pacific University's founding, though it was never published.

As for the president, as early as 1944, the *Heart of Oak* notes that the "amiable, witty, clever" Giersbach "spent most of the school year traveling throughout the States" in his attempt to raise funds "to keep Pacific alive in a deadened world." Giersbach's absences became the butt of good-natured jokes in subsequent yearbooks, and his schedule became even more hectic when circumstances surrounding the untimely death of Republican Governor Douglas McKay in 1952 resulted in Giersbach being appointed to the Oregon State Senate in the following year. While Giersbach was moderately successful on the funding front, he was apparently not amiable, witty, or clever enough to appease the faculty, who, increasingly disgruntled at his absenteeism, finally sent a resolution to the Board of Trustees calling for his resignation. After holding hearings, the Trustees summarily sacked Giersbach in mid-year 1953.

Upon Giersbach's departure, Pacific managed to muddle through for seven months

A Football Legend and His Son

WHEN PACIFIC UNIVERSITY hired Dr. Paul Stagg to be the new athletic director and head football coach in 1947, it connected the school with one of the game's legendary figures: Amos Alonzo Stagg (1862–1965). The elder Stagg, known as "Lonny" to his friends, shaped the game of football from its beginnings in the 1890s when it caught on as a popular sport. Known as the "Grand Old Man of Football," Lonny Stagg earned the title as a result of his 41 years as coach for the University of Chicago. Not ready to retire in 1933 when he was 70, he took another coaching job at the College of the Pacific in California, and stayed there until 1946. At age 85 he took yet another job as football coach at Susquehanna University in Pennsylvania, finally retiring five years later. He was the oldest active coach in the United States and had the highest number of coaching seasons in history. Over the span of his 59-year coaching career, Amos Alonzo Stagg contributed more to football's development as a sport than any other individual. He is credited with such innovations as the forward pass, the T-formation, the Statue of Liberty play, the place kick, the lateral and hidden-ball plays, slip-proof jerseys, padded uniforms, and the tackling dummy.

Coach Paul Stagg (left)

This celebrity status did not go unnoticed when, on occasion, Lonny Stagg came to Forest Grove to help his son Paul with his coaching duties, usually during spring training. Paul Stagg had come to Pacific with solid academic credentials from New York University (Ph.D. in physical education), Columbia University (master's degree), and the University of Chicago (B.S.). He stayed at Pacific University for 13 years, building a strong athletic program and a respectable football record. Under his guidance, the Badgers enjoyed a record of 65 wins, 53 losses, and 7 ties. During the 1949–1952 period Pacific emerged as a powerhouse in the Northwest Conference. Stagg's teams won co-championships in 1949, 1951, and 1952. They even won the Pear Bowl in 1949.

Ironically, when Paul Stagg resigned in 1961, he headed south to coach at the University of the Pacific (the name had by then been changed from "College" to "University"), assuming his father's former position there. Though he never attained the stature of his famous father, Paul Stagg became and remains a legend to Badger boosters who remember the glory days of football at Pacific.

Dr. Charles J. Armstrong, president of Pacific University from 1953–1958

without a president before appointing Charles Armstrong, a Harvard Ph.D. and, at the time, administrative dean at Whitman College. In his inaugural address, delivered on the 100th anniversary of Pacific's being granted its charter as a college, Armstrong came out strongly for higher academic standards, greater athletic spirit, a close-knit institutional community, and, as always, the importance of the liberal arts:

> As [John Stewart] Mill said, "Men are men before they are lawyers or physicians or manufacturers; and if you make them capable and sensible men they will make themselves capable and sensible lawyers or physicians." … We are confirmed in our belief that liberal education is the best preparation for meaningful adult activity, for leading a better life and making a better living.

As we shall see later, the role of the liberal arts would become increasingly thorny as Pacific's professional programs flourished, but on most of the matters that Armstrong raised in his address, he managed to deliver. By the end of his five-year tenure, academic standards had improved to a point where three-quarters of the incoming freshman were from the top half of their high school graduating classes. Faculty morale was up as well, thanks in great part to Armstrong's support of policies for tenure, promotion, leave, and retirement. Under the able chairmanship of George Rossman, associate justice of the Oregon Supreme Court, the Board of Trustees worked with Armstrong and the faculty to bolster enrollment, selectivity, and a sound athletic program.

Like graduates of the late '40s, students from the Armstrong years left with a strong sense of loyalty, manifested in sending many of their children to Pacific and continuing to support the university as alumni. Distinguished graduates from the period include Jason Boe, '55, who became president of the Oregon State Senate, and William Young, '58, who served as director of the Oregon Department of Environmental Quality.

Despite these important advances, however,

the campus of 1959 (the year Armstrong departed to assume the presidency at the University of Nevada) did not look the part of a modern university. Operating on an annual budget of about $800,000, Armstrong had managed to get additional funds to finance the Judith Scott Walter dormitory in 1958 (named after the daughter of Pacific's first graduate, Harvey Scott) and to remodel Knight Hall—a dormitory at the time—for use by the Music Department. Other than this, the only structures added to the campus during the combined presidencies of Armstrong and Giersbach were U.S. Army surplus barracks. Most visitors to Pacific would likely have agreed with the visiting presidential candidate who characterized the condition of Pacific's facilities as "lamentable." That visiting candidate was Miller A. F. Ritchie, who would become the primary agent for turning this situation around.

A MOMENT OF DECISION

The hiring of Miller Ritchie as president of Pacific University in 1959 (he did not officially assume office until 1960) has an element of *déjà vu*. As we saw earlier, when Pacific's first president, Sidney Harper Marsh, was offered the post in Forest Grove, he wrote to George Atkinson: "My lungs are proving themselves too sensitive for this climate, and for a few days especially I have been thinking that migration to Florida or some warmer climate would be better than remaining here." Like Marsh, Ritchie was living in New York when he got word of the opening at Pacific, had recently been considering a move to Florida, and was persuaded to come to Oregon largely because the climate might be beneficial to a respiratory condition—in this case, that of his eight-year-old daughter, Betsy. Marsh, however, had accepted the offer immediately and with no idea of what he was getting into. Ritchie was more cautious—and with good reason.

Before coming to Pacific, Ritchie had spent six years as president of Hartwick College in Oneonta, New York, a position he had accepted on "a funny religious feeling of obligation." As he notes in his book *The College Presidency: Ini-*

Judith Scott Walter Hall was named after the daughter (above) of Pacific's first graduate, Harvey Scott.

Left: Jane Gould, '60, Gartha Ferrant, '59, and Ginny Cooper, '59 meet in one of Walter Hall's dormitory rooms in October 1958.

Knight Hall was renovated in 1958 for use by the music department.

Pictured in the spring of 1958, after the dedication of Judith Scott Walter Hall, are (left to right) Justice George Rossman, trustee; Mrs. John Carruthers, daughter of Judith Scott Walter; Dr. Charles Armstrong, president; and Mr. Russell Walter and Mrs. John Anderson, son and second daughter of the philanthropist.

tiation into the Order of the Turtle: "I should have asked for the annual reports of the past five years. If I had read them, I certainly would not have taken the job." When considering the Pacific offer, therefore, he did take a careful look both at the campus and at the annual reports, concluding that "Pacific's institutional illness was chronic, not acute" and that the financial state of the college was one of "lethargy and defeatism." He summarized:

> The almost continuous deficits for many years past, the lamentable condition of the buildings, the obvious inadequacy of the faculty and administrative staff, numerically and otherwise, were eloquently persuasive in the negative direction.

Despite this assessment, Ritchie ultimately decided to take the job, but only after a second visit to the campus and considerable wavering. What finally swayed him, in addition to considerations of his daughter's health, was the solid Board of Trustees that President Armstrong had put together, which included (in addition to Oregon Supreme Court Justice George Rossman) Thomas Delzell, chairman of the board of the Portland General Electric Company, and Robert Hansberger, new president of Boise Cascade. Ritchie's acceptance of the post on the eve of the most tumultuous decade in the history of U.S. college campuses—the 1960s—would prove pivotal to the future of Pacific University.

LOOKING THE PART: THE RITCHIE DECADE

While Ritchie's contributions to Pacific would not be limited to expanding the physical facilities, before-and-after photos of the campus show a remarkable and dramatic difference. With a seed grant of $100,000 from the Congregational Board of Home Missions, Ritchie launched a $10 million development program that would transform the campus. "Launched" may be the wrong word, since the announced plan initially raised more eyebrows than money. As one of the alumni remembers it:

The inauguration of Pacific's 12th president, M. A. F. Ritchie (second from left). Guests included Governor William F. Quinn of Hawaii (left), Board of Trustees Chair Judge George Rossman (second from right), and Governor Mark Hatfield of Oregon (Quinn and Hatfield received honorary degrees).

Right: Ritchie at his desk in Marsh Hall, 1960

"Many students, and perhaps more secretly, many faculty members, regarded this ambitious plan skeptically as far too unrealistic to ever find realization."

But find realization it did. A mere listing of the additions and renovations between 1960 and 1970 encompasses many of the large, signature buildings that grace the campus today:

Washburne Hall *(aka the University Center)*, 1963;

Clark Hall *(a coed residence hall)*, 1966;

Jefferson Hall, Brombach Wing *(College of Optometry)*, 1967;

Harvey W. Scott Memorial Library, 1967;

Aquatic Center *(jointly with City of Forest Grove)*, 1968;

Adult Student Housing *(100 apartments)*, 1969;

Pacific Athletic Center, 1970.

To put all this in perspective, more construction occurred on campus during the 10 years of Ritchie's tenure than in the previous 100 years. In those same 10 years, the annual budget went from one to three million dollars, financial aid leapt from $100,00 to $950,000, faculty salaries increased almost 100%, tuition rose from $550 to $1,350, the endowment doubled to $4 million, and enrollment shot up from 707 to 1,209. In all, Ritchie raised $11 million in government loans and grants, foundation bequests, and private gifts.

He also built on President Armstrong's work by adding other prominent figures to the Board of Trustees: Senator Wayne Morse; Ronald McCreight, vice president of Jantzen, Inc., who chaired the board; and Ralph Shumm of the U.S. National Bank of Oregon, who served as board secretary throughout the decade. As a result of these combined efforts, Pacific University emerged from the '60s a modern university complex with a strong governing body and total assets of $10.8 million, almost three times those of a decade earlier.

But campus development is not what we generally associate with college life in the turbulent '60s, and Pacific had its share of politi-

In 1970 the Pacific Athletic Center, serving as an anchor on the north side of the campus, was opened to replace the gymnasium built in 1910.

cal unrest. Here too, however, Ritchie's leadership style proved decisive. When the inevitable cries of a communication gap went up, Ritchie resisted the temptation to be confrontational and adopted a radical stance for university presidents of the time: he listened. Recognizing student unrest for what it was—a search for values—Ritchie at the end of his tenure in 1970 described the students of the Vietnam War era as "far more intellectual than my generation of the 1930s," noting: "They may not be as respectful of set rules of conduct, but they are more concerned about problems of social significance. They are committed to a search for a better world."

Such an attitude, as historian James Hitchman puts it, "had the effect of making Pacific an exciting but not an embattled place in the 1960s." The later Vietnam War years would witness a visit to campus by activist Dick Gregory and participation in the Vietnam Moratorium, but student protests were mild by comparison to those on other campuses. The pages of the *Index* crackled with student concerns, but no one, for example, attempted to occupy Marsh Hall, and anti-war demonstrations were considerably more orderly than the traditional "Boxer" tosses.

As for internal unrest, the students' demands, if not always met, were taken seriously. The '60s saw the initation of course credit by

Above: A 1965 campus scene with part of Old College Hall in the background (it was moved to this position in 1963) and Herrick Hall Right: Students painted the old gymnasium prior to demolition in 1970-71. Washburne Hall is visible in the background.

examination, a pass/fail grading system, and Black Studies (by the mid-'70s Pacific would have one of the highest percentages of non-White students of any college on the West Coast). When, in 1969, the students demanded open dormitories, the administration responded by allowing students over 21 to live off-campus and by establishing less restrictive hours for those living on campus. Even the rules for smoking were relaxed, though drinking on campus remained forbidden.

After ably seeing the college through the most active period in the university's history, Miller Ritchie left in 1970 to accept a position at the University of Miami, Florida, returning to Oregon in 1975. He and his wife, Josephine, have remained active in campus affairs and activities, serving on various committees and vounteering time and expertise to support such campus groups as Friends of the Library, Friends of Music, and Friends of Old College Hall. Their daughter Betsy, incidentally, whose respiratory condition played such an major part in bringing Ritchie to Pacific, thrived in the

Oregon climate and, the mother of two, currently works as a nurse in a Catholic hospital in Washington County.

We cannot close the Ritchie decade, however, without taking note of an event that looms large in the memories of many Pacific alumni. In the fall of 1969, "Boxer," the original Chinese incense-burner that had first made its memorable appearance on campus in 1898, disappeared, apparently for good. Only a year earlier, the student body had voted that this college curio should replace the "Badger" as the official school mascot, an honor it holds even to the present day. And while the statuette had previously disappeared for short periods and had by now lost several of its appendages, it would be sorely missed. Passionate appeals for the return of "The College Spirit," Boxer's original name, would periodically surface in the *Index* and elsewhere for many years to come, but to no avail. It may be fitting, however, that Boxer's arrival and departure on campus coincide with two of the most memorable decades in Pacific University's long history.

The Last "Boxer Rebellion"

*I*N 1969, Pacific's original beloved "Boxer" disappeared from campus and has not been back since. The context out of which the disappearance evolved included a number of confrontations between members of the Black Student Union (BSU) and other segments of the student body. Some of the latter resented the idea that black students needed their own student union, while the black students felt alienated and invisible on campus. A former BSU member recalls that Ralph Ellison's *Invisible Man* was required

reading at the time, and alluded to this by way of explaining the motivation for taking Boxer: "What we were saying to them is: You don't see us, but you sure see that dog, so we're going to take that dog and you won't see it any more." Boxer, in fact, was not a "dog," but the alumnus' point is forcefully made.

One of the last "Boxer tosses" before Boxer disappeared in 1969

At approximately 9:00 on a Friday morning in the fall of 1969, a group of BSU members was on its way to class when, in front of Old College Hall, they passed a massive pile of white male students wrestling for possession of Boxer, which had been flashed by members of Alpha Zeta fraternity. As the black students walked by, they commented to one another how stupid it was to put so much value on "that dog," but proceeded to their classes.

When they returned by the same route around 2:00 in the afternoon, the struggle was still going on, but by now the white students looked considerably worse for wear. It was at this point that the black students decided to take Boxer as an act of protest about their status, or lack of same, on campus. Even then, they had time to go back to their rooms, some of which were off campus, and change into grubby clothes before returning to the scene of the melee.

One of them was instructed to wait on Pacific Avenue in a car. The others—there were approximately 15 of them—went back to the scene of the scuffle, managed to wrest Boxer from the weary participants, and made a dash for the get-away car. Pursued, they tossed Boxer back and forth until one of them finally pitched it through an open window of the car, which sped away. This was the last time that Boxer was seen on campus.

Boxer's fate after this is sketchy, and none of the participants in the heist seems to know of its present whereabouts. It left the country at one point, spent some time in Europe, and may have found its way to the Phillipines. There have been rumors about it being melted down or thrown off the Golden Gate Bridge, but none of these rumors has been verified.

Placed in context, the disappearance of Boxer is a telling footnote to the often turbulent attempt in the late '60s to integrate African-Americans into the mainstream of university life. In 1965, there were only five black students at Pacific; in the following year there were 16 and, in 1970, more than 60. By the mid-'70s, Pacific had one of the highest percentages of non-white students of any college on the West Coast.

Aftermath of the '60s:
Life on a Modern Campus

The light shines in the darkness. — PACIFIC UNIVERSITY'S MOTTO, 1982–1983

W HEN JAMES MILLER, former academic dean at Otterbein College in Ohio, succeeded Miller Ritchie as president of Pacific in 1970, he had a hard act to follow. Almost inevitably, Miller's impact on the campus would be less dramatic than that of his predecessor, but it would be no less important. While the country pondered the Watergate hearings that led to the downfall of the Nixon administration, the Miller administration pondered the twin realities of mounting inflation and dwindling Federal support. Fiscal responsibility, coupled with improved academic standing, would be the major objectives of the Miller years (1970–1983)—and the major achievements.

FRIENDLY BICKERING: CAREERS THROUGH THE LIBERAL ARTS?

1970 was a watershed year for American college-age youth. It was a year that began with the U.S. invasion of Cambodia, which set off a powder keg of campus protests, culminating in the National Guard killing of four students at Kent State University. It ended with the court martial of Lt. William Calley for his leadership role in the slaughter of 102 civilians in My Lai, South Vietnam, and the Supreme Court ruling that, in effect, if 18-year-olds were old enough to kill and be killed as a result of U.S. policy, then they were old enough to vote and have a voice in that policy.

As the decade wore on, however, university administrators across the country began to re-examine the increased voice of students in school policy. Besides being cumbersome, student participation in academic matters put an increasing strain on what many faculty saw as the philosophical underpinnings of a university education.

This was especially true at small, private, liberal arts institutions like Pacific University. And while the addition, in 1975, of the School of Physical Therapy bolstered Pacific's status as a university, it simultaneously threatened those who were already concerned about the diminishing status of the liberal arts. Indeed, the very question of whether Pacific could reasonably call itself a "liberal arts college" began to elicit a passion reminiscent of earlier debates about the sectarian identity of the school.

For example, one of the innovations of James Miller's administration would be a new curriculum called a "7-7-3." Under this novel teaching structure, influenced by developments at Colorado College, the fall and spring terms consisted of two seven-week courses followed by a three-week course (Pacific's current "Winter III" is a vestige of this system). Faculty typically taught two courses a term, and students took two three-credit courses each term. Students also took one-credit experiential courses, of which science laboratories were a major fea-

James Miller

ture. After three years of on-campus study, a student could take a fourth year of applied study off-campus in the form of an internship at such places as Tektronix, IBM, Veterans' Hospital, and the Oregon Primate Center.

While this arrangement proved popular with students, its implications were not lost on those faculty who felt that the rug was being pulled out from under the liberal arts. The rise and fall of the 7-7-3 system tells us much about the terms of James Miller and Robert Duvall. Among the new curriculum's more outspoken critics was Professor Ted Sizer, director of the theater department from 1964–76. Interviewed by the *Index* in his final year at Pacific, Sizer pulled no punches:

> I don't think the 7-7-3 is worth a damn. I think we have gone too far in designing courses to meet the individual interests of the student ... . We're looking more like a trade school, and we're working with students, preparing them for a job and not life ... . If we follow the lead of the community colleges, we shouldn't charge Cadillac prices and turn out a Pinto.

For the record, a new Cadillac El Dorado in 1975 cost $10,875, while the tuition at Pacific for that year was $2,365—low even by community college standards. But Sizer's point is clear enough. And while the language differs considerably, the sentiment hearkens back to one expressed by Pacific's first president, Sidney Harper Marsh, in an address to the Gamma Sigma Society in April of 1868:

> While most truly practical, [a college education] is not narrow and mercenary; it is not merely in order to enable the possessor to make money. ... It is not to fit the youth for position or honor or wealth, but to fit him so that he may be the most in any position whatever.

This, of course, is the classic statement of the liberal arts ideal, which, according to Sizer and others at Pacific in the '70s, was being reduced to little more than lip service. Recog-

nizing the potential for conflict, the administration tried to accommodate all parties by adopting the slogan "Careers Through the Liberal Arts."

But money speaks louder than slogans, and the bottom line was that the professional programs, and especially the College of Optometry, bore the lion's share of the burden for keeping the university solvent: the university endowment accounted for a mere three percent of the annual income; Federal support supplied another 18 percent; the balance came from tuition and the clinics, mainly from the College of Optometry. From this point of view, the recurrent demand from the optometry faculty for salaries more in line with those of comparable professional schools was reasonable enough, though it did not always seem so to their colleagues in the College of Arts and Sciences.

This is not to suggest that the respective faculties were in open warfare. For one thing, Harold Haynes of the College of Optometry, who was president of the faculty at this time, was a strong advocate for the arts and sciences, and did an admirable job of bridging the gap between the various factions. For another, universities are by nature civil places and—as Miller Ritchie once put it—folks at Pacific "are a pretty level-headed lot." Also, as sociologist Pat Marchand has noted, "Friendly bickering is one of the signs of a healthy community." Marchand might have added that it is also a sign of a democratic community. Part of what Pacific University was experiencing was a shift from the paradigm of the college president as charismatic leader and ultimate decision-maker to one in which power is more properly diffused throughout the community—at least in theory. To feel disenfranchised assumes an expectation that one's voice and vote should matter.

President Miller, both by temperament and philosophy, encouraged this expectation among the faculty. As with any transition administrator, however, Miller is remembered with mixed feelings: some recall him as a relatively ineffective "caretaker" president between two activists—Miller Ritchie and Robert Duvall; others feel his laid-back, participatory style of leadership reflected a higher degree of respect for the faculty. This discrepancy, which hinges in part on whether one places a greater value on process or on results, is not one that hindsight is likely to resolve.

FULFILLING THE DREAMS

As for results, James Hitchman, in his history of liberal arts colleges in Oregon and Washington, observes that "Between 1977 and 1980, Pacific began to fulfill its dreams." The statistics bear this out. Between these years the grade point average of entering freshmen rose from 2.6 to 3.2 as enrollment hit the 1,200 mark. By the end of the decade 60 percent of the faculty in the College of Arts and Sciences held doctorates—compared to a mere 25 percent as late as 1950. The total faculty produced more than 145 books and articles between 1978 and 1980.

Several faculty distinguished themselves in other ways as well. Professor H. C. "Hap" Hingston, besides publishing two textbooks in the field of speech, was named Speaker of the Year by the Oregon Speech Association in 1972, and served as president of the Western Forensic Association. Another professor of speech, Dr. Fred Scheller, was appointed to the Board for World Ministry of the United Church of Christ, which the Oregon Congregationalists had joined in 1963. Optometry professor William Ludlam became a member of the Oregon State Commission for the Blind. The National Science Foundation funded several research projects carried on by Pacific faculty members. Despite the internal squabbles, faculty morale at Pacific University was probably higher during this period than it had been at any time since the McClelland decade.

The '70s also witnessed the fulfillment of Pacific's dreams on the baseball field. Coach Chuck Bafaro led the Boxer nine to a league championship in '72 and repeated the feat with back-to-back championships in '78 and '79.

Theatre professor "Hap" Hingston was named Speaker of the Year by the Oregon Speech Association in 1972.

Bafaro, who coached from 1963–1994 and remains something of a legend on campus, was inducted to the National Association of Intercollegiate Athletics Hall of Fame in 1979.

The wrestling team, under the leadership of mathematics professor and coach Mike Clock, also rose to prominence during the '70s. In fact, after losing every dual wrestling event in 1967, Clock's first year as coach, Pacific's wrestling squad went on to win every conference title from 1968 through 1984, the year the Northwest Conference in wrestling disbanded. The 1976 and 1977 teams were among the top 10 at the national level, and in 1978 Rick Franklin, '78, became the first Pacific wrestler to win an individual national championship. Wrestling at Pacific would reach its zenith in 1982 when the school hosted the national tournament, an event that drew a crowd of some 3,000 people.

Financially, too, the university began to prosper. The Murdock Charitable Trust gave $750,000 in response to Pacific's managing to raise $3 million in three years, half of which went to erecting a new chemistry building. Alumni support increased to 25 percent, or about $80,000 annually. Assistance from the trustees grew as well, and by 1980 the endowment had risen to $5 million. Throughout his

Above: Nobel Laureate Linus Pauling was the speaker at the dedication of the chemistry building. Right: Charles and Edith Hansen McGill (both class of 1930) for whom McGill auditorium is named, were honored by President Miller at the dedication in 1982.

tenure, President Miller had to race to keep up with inflation, but he had plenty of support, and the effort was paying off.

IMPORTANT SYMBOLS

One of James Miller's last acts as president turned out to be one of the most controversial as well. In 1982, he changed the motto of Pacific University from *Pro Christo et Regno Ejus* to *Lux in Tenebris Lucet*—"The Light Shines in the Darkness." The former motto, it will be recalled, had been chosen in 1886 by Rev. Jacob Ellis, one of Pacific's less illustrious presidents and one who had unsuccessfully lobbied for strong sectarian control. The Congregationalist—indeed, even the Christian—nature of the university had long since ceased to be a volatile issue, and Miller had reasonable grounds for assuming that the explicit reference to "Christ and His Kingdom" would not be missed.

He was wrong. Ironically, the Biblical text (John 1.1) from which Miller's motto was taken is, "The light shines in the darkness, and the darkness does not comprehend it." Whether out of Christian fervor or mere respect for tradition, the Pacific community did not comprehend the need for the change.

When Robert Duvall assumed the presidency in 1983, one of his first acts would be to restore the old motto, demonstrating once again that while Pacific University might waver on other points, it has never lacked for pride in its history.

Finally, the '70s also provided Pacific the opportunity to demonstrate yet another of its most salient character traits—resiliency. In April 1975, a fire broke out in Marsh Memorial Hall when the wooden casings around the hot water pipes overheated and burst into flames. By the time the fire had run its course, the entire building had been gutted.

Byron Steiger, a newly hired faculty member at the time, recalls that the only copies of his uncompleted doctoral dissertation were in a metal file cabinet in his office when the fire broke out. In the conflagration, the file cabinet fell three floors to the basement, where it was found the next day by firemen digging through the rubble. Amazingly, the flames had gone around the file cabinet, and Steiger's manuscript survived unscathed.

Others were not so lucky. The highly combustible microfiche on which many records were stored had fed the fire, leaving the Admissions Office without any application ma-

Left: Marsh Hall after the devastating fire in 1975
Below: Football and the accompanying bonfire remained Homecoming traditions until the football program was ended in 1992; today Homecoming continues as an opportunity for alumni to return to campus and meet old friends.

terials from incoming freshmen. Again amazingly, the admissions personnel managed to reconstruct the system, a feat that entailed tracking down all the applicants and having them resubmit their application materials.

Those who remember old Marsh Hall at this time confirm that it was not an easy place to work. One faculty member describes it as "Dickensian," with bare light bulbs, small teaching rooms, and few amenities. Still, the loss of the campus' most cherished landmark was significant, both symbolically and financially. Undaunted, however, the trustees hired the firm of Martin, Soderstrom, and Matteson to remodel the structure over a two-year period. While retaining the design and feel of the original building, present-day Marsh Hall, with its tasteful combination of brick, glass, and tongue-in-groove wood paneling, stands as a modern monument to its namesake, and to all those whose "acts of splendid audacity" have kept his vision alive.

The Professional Schools

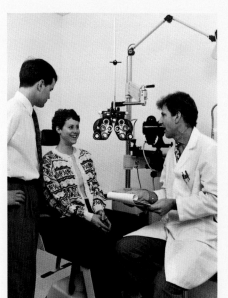

*G*IVEN SIDNEY HARPER MARSH'S preoccupation with vision, it seems fitting that the first major add-on to "the house that Marsh built" should be a college of optometry. Fitting too, in light of Pacific's origins, was the serendipitous nature of the circumstances that led to such a choice, which in turn greatly influenced the development of future professional programs at Pacific. All of the present professional schools at Pacific—even, one could argue, the School of Education—focus on various aspects of physical or psychological health, reinforcing the Congregationalist subscription to the ancient credo of "a sound mind in a sound body."

The current structure of the professional schools reflects a long and varied process of innovation and reorganization. In 1983, a division of the Health Sciences was created, consisting of the Departments of Physical Therapy, Occupational Therapy, Therapeutic Recreation, and Communication Disorders. By 1989 the departments of Therapeutic Recreation and Communication Disorders had been closed and the School of Professional Psychology had joined the university. The continued growth of the physical and occupational therapy programs led to them being constituted as free-standing schools. Thus, in May 1989 the schools of optometry, physical therapy, occupational therapy, and professional psychology were organized into the Faculty of the Health Professions. In 1995 with the addition of the School of Education, the group was renamed—Faculty of Professional Schools. The most recent addition to Pacific's professional programs is the School of Physician Assistant Studies, which came on board in 1997.

PHYSICAL THERAPY

Prior to the initiation of Pacific University's Physical Therapy Program in 1975, Oregon did not have a program for educating professional physical therapists. Even now, almost a quarter-of-a-century later, Pacific has the only such program in the state.

In the early 1970s, Varina French, a professor in the physical education department, and David Malcolm, dean of the College of Arts and Sciences, began to plan for a program in physical therapy with the cooperation of the Oregon Physical Therapy Association. Jean Baldwin was hired as the first academic administrator of the new department, which was located in the Natural Sciences Division and housed in the Pacific University athletic complex.

The first class, consisting of 16 students, matriculated in September 1975 and graduated in May 1977. In that same year, the program received accreditation from the American Physical Therapy Association and the department was moved to the basement of McCormick Hall. In August 1987 it moved to its present location, the Physical Therapy Building.

The program originally consisted of three years of undergraduate work followed by an intensive 21-month professional course of study leading to a bachelor of science degree. In 1985, the program was redesigned as an entry-level master's program leading to the degree of Master of Science in Physical Therapy. The current format is three years undergraduate work followed by three academic years of professional work. The class of 1988 was the first to graduate with this new degree.

In keeping with the university's long-standing spirit of community service, the master's degree integrates clinical and didactic study. Instead of leaving clinical education to follow the academic portion of the program, full-time clinicals are initiated in the second semester of the first year and progress to longer affiliations every semester thereafter. Contracts with 145 clinical sites are maintained for internships and clinical experience. Over the years, a clinic was opened to serve the faculty, students, and staff of Pacific as well as the local community.

Currently, the School of Physical Therapy boasts nine full-time faculty members, six part-time instructors, and many guest lecturers. By now, Pacific has more than 600 physical therapy alumni, in addition to the enrolled 108 students.

OCCUPATIONAL THERAPY

The occupational therapy (OT) program at Pacific University was established in the fall of 1984, though the process of developing such a program in the state of Oregon dates back to 1948, when members of the Occupational Therapy Association of Oregon (OTAO) pre-

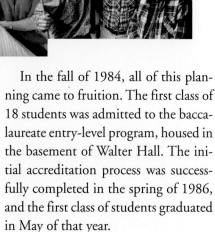

sented data from a needs assessment to several state institutions of higher education. At that time, none of the schools was interested in beginning procedures for developing an occupational therapy program. Jean Vann, Virginia Hatch, and Shirley Bowing were just a few of the therapists who invested time and energy over the years toward developing a professional program in Oregon.

In 1976, Pacific University contacted the American Occupational Therapy Association to explore the possibility of establishing a baccalaureate entry-level program. Sue Nelson, president of the OTAO, met with Dean Malcomb of Pacific's College of Arts and Sciences. An advisory committee was appointed by the state association to assist the college in exploring the possibility of developing a program. After some consideration, however, the issue was once again tabled as unfeasible.

In 1979, Lilian Crawford and Kay Rhoney approached Pacific University in hope of reactivating the issue. A task force, chaired by Dr. Tom Griffith of Pacific's Science Division, enthusiastically worked with the OTAO on a proposal to begin a professional occupational therapy program. This proposal was finally presented to, and approved by, the Faculty Senate in January 1983, with subsequent approval granted by the Curriculum Committee and the Board of Trustees.

In the fall of 1984, all of this planning came to fruition. The first class of 18 students was admitted to the baccalaureate entry-level program, housed in the basement of Walter Hall. The initial accreditation process was successfully completed in the spring of 1986, and the first class of students graduated in May of that year.

Over the years, the School of OT has continued to grow and develop. In May 1991, the school completed its second accreditation process, being cited for a "cutting edge curriculum" in occupational therapy. During the 1994–95 academic year, the School of OT was directed to develop a proposal for implementing a master's entry-level program, ultimately phasing out the existing baccalaureate entry-level program. The proposed plan was approved in May 1996. The last baccalaureate entry-level class of students entered in fall 1996; the first master's entry-level students began in fall 1997 and will graduate in 2000.

PROFESSIONAL PSYCHOLOGY

The School of Professional Psychology was developed over a five-year period beginning in 1975, when a group of Oregon psychologists joined to explore the prospects of a doctoral training program for professional psychologists. Spurred by the lack of training opportunities for professional psychologists in the Northwest, the founding committee incorporated in the State of Oregon as a nonprofit educational institution on December 31, 1975. The School began operations and admitted the first class in September 1979.

Known then as the Oregon Graduate School of Professional Psychology (OGSPP), the school was initially authorized by the Oregon Educational Coordinating Commission to grant the doctor of psychology (Psy.D.) degree. When the school joined Pacific University in 1985, it became accredited by the Northwest Association of Schools and Colleges. (Don Rushmer was president of OGSPP and became a Pacific University trustee at the time of the merger, and was later named provost and vice president for academic affairs at Pacific.) In 1989 the school changed its name to the School of Professional Psychology and, a year later, was accredited by the American Psychological Association.

Like all of Pacific's professional schools, the School of Professional Psychology is committed to serving the community as it trains its students. At the school's Psychological Service Center in Portland, which serves as the primary training center, students provide an array of quality psychological services to the greater Portland area under the supervision of licensed, experienced psychologists. As has been true since the school's

inception, students also receive training at various approved community sites.

In 1991, the School of Professional Psychology started offering a Master of Science degree in Clinical Psychology, as well as the Psy.D. degree. This master's degree is designed to prepare students for eventual doctoral training in clinical psychology. In 1999 the school added a third degree, a Master of Arts in Counseling Psychology, which is designed to prepare students to practice in the community.

The school's history has been one of continuing efforts to become established, and to develop into a mature organization, offering excellent training and valuable service to the community.

SCHOOL OF EDUCATION

Tabitha Brown's vision established a rich tradition and foundation for Pacific University's leadership in teacher education. In order to care for the "poor children"—those orphaned by the Oregon Trail or left behind for the California gold rush—she used her teaching experiences and began to teach other teachers. A century and a half later, Pacific University continues this tradition, maintaining a strong reputation for its teacher education programs.

In 1911, the Oregon Legislature authorized the State Superintendent of Public Instruction to issue teaching certificates to qualified college graduates, authorizing them to teach in high schools; the law further required that high school teachers be certified college graduates. Following an inspection by the United States Bureau of Education, Pacific University was one of only three institutions in Oregon to be granted the privilege of teacher accreditation at that time. Throughout most of the century, the certificate program consisted of a

Bachelor of Arts degree with a major in Education. In 1989, however, Pacific was the first university in Oregon to receive approval from the state licensing agency to offer a fifth-year master's degree program.

Pacific established a second site for teacher preparation in Eugene, Oregon in 1992. This Lane County campus currently licenses approximately the same number of teachers each year as the Forest Grove campus. Between the two sites, Pacific University has become one of the leading teacher preparation institutions in the state.

Until recently, the teacher education programs were organized within a Division of Education of the College of Arts and Sciences. In 1994, however, the governance structure was re-organized and the School of Education was established as an academic unit with the autonomy to meet the specific needs of preparing professional teachers. Today's programs, recently redesigned as a result of extensive research and a study of school reform in Oregon and the nation, have been structured around the faculty's vision of the competencies to be attained by the graduates of the School of Education.

PHYSICIAN ASSISTANT STUDIES

In 1994, the Board of Trustees of Pacific University created an ad hoc committee on the health professions. This committee, which has since become a standing committee of the board, was charged with three functions, one of which was to consider the initiation of new programs in the health professions at Pacific.

In the fall of that same year, the Career Development Office of Pacific University held a health career seminar. This seminar included a presentation about the physician assistant profession, including the possibility of starting such a program at Pacific University. At that time, there was not a single Physician Assistant (PA) program in the state of Oregon. In March 1995, after careful evaluation of the various options, the Board Committee on the Health Professions gave the go-ahead to develop a physician assistant program.

In early 1995, Dr. Donald Rushmer, the university provost and vice president for academic affairs, hired a consultant and began the process of meeting with physician assistants in the community. In October of that year, having determined that the demand for PAs justified the development of a program, the university enlisted Rod Hooker, a PA researcher at the Kaiser Permanente Center for Health Research, to conduct a feasibility study that further assessed the distribution and need for PAs in Oregon. The study demonstrated that Oregon was understaffed by physician assistants when compared to other states, and estimated the capacity for additional PAs in Oregon over the next decade to be in the 300–500 range.

In fall 1995, a national search began for a program director, resulting in the selection of Christine Legler, who joined the faculty in July 1996. In the interim, Dr. Rushmer and the PA consultant continued to identify potential clinical training sites, developed a curriculum and list of prerequisites, and held meetings with the PA Curriculum and Advisory committees to further develop the program.

Establishment of the School of Physician Assistant Studies was authorized by the Board of Trustees on December 14, 1995. The school's first class of students was admitted in June of 1997 and graduated in August of 1999.

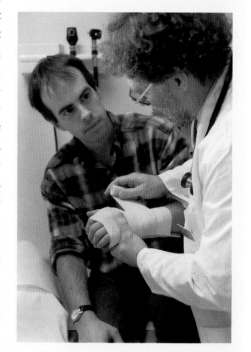

Increased Visibility:
Courting the Larger Community

[President] Duvall told the Pacific story better than anyone—better than Miller, better than Ritchie. But that didn't give him the right to cut football.

— A PACIFIC UNIVERSITY ALUMNUS

*A*S THE ABOVE OBSERVATION about Pacific University's 14th president suggests, Robert Duvall's tenure at Pacific (1983–1995) played to mixed reviews. Duvall's overriding goal as president was to broaden the university's horizons beyond the Forest Grove community. In this, he was extending the seminal work of Miller Ritchie, who, in recalling his time at Pacific, had complained: "The thought that Pacific University's community really is the greater Portland metropolitan area seemed never to have entered anyone's head." It entered Duvall's head soon enough and would become what most consider the signature theme of his presidency.

PROMISING START

Robert Duvall came to Pacific University from Rollins College in Florida, an institution that, like Pacific, had been founded by transplanted New England Congregationalists. Like Sidney Harper Marsh, one of Duvall's heroes, the new president was deeply rooted in academia: his father was a college professor (Whitworth), as were two of his brothers. Like Marsh, too, he would be an aggressive promoter of Pacific, whose administrative style was considered by some to be a tad high-handed compared to that of his predecessor, James Miller. While Duvall was not philosophically opposed to the democratization of power, he was impatient with the process that this implied and, when push came to shove, tended to prefer efficiency of action over consensus of opinion.

One of Duvall's first changes was to hire Seth Singleton as dean of the Arts and Sciences. A current faculty member sympathetic to the Duvall regime recalls: "Seth was confident, bright, had a 'can-do' attitude, and was very charismatic. When he came on the stage, things took off." Duvall and Singleton shared a conviction that the way ahead lay with increased enrollments and energetic new faculty. The central strategy was that Pacific should not seek to emulate the state universities, but should try to compete head-to-head with Lewis and Clark, Reed, and other private colleges in the Northwest.

The year Duvall arrived on campus, 1983, coincided with the enactment of the Solomon Amendment, under which all students who applied for Federal financial assistance were required to sign a compliance form stating that they had either registered with the Selective Service, or were not required by law to do so. Though the amendment turned out to be something of a tempest in a teapot, it did

Robert Duvall came to Pacific as president in 1983 and served 12 years.

The End of a Long Tradition

EVENTS LEADING UP to the demise of football as a sport at Pacific included both the comic and the tragic. In the former category, the Boxer football team made the national news when, in a game against Linfield College, one of the Pacific players ran off the bench to tackle a Linfield linebacker who had broken loose and was streaking downfield on the way to a touchdown. While this lapse of sportsmanship pleased the fans, it failed to amuse those who were already beginning to feel that Pacific's football recruitment efforts were compromising academic standards.

On the tragic side, a Pacific player named Eric Ross '92 was seriously injured during a football game and, after two years in a coma, died as a result of head injuries. A plaque on "Eric's Way" in Trombley Square commemorates the loss of this popular student.

All of this, combined with what some considered the exorbitant cost of running the football program, led to the inevitable decision. On February 27, 1992, the trustees voted 17-5 to drop football as a sport at Pacific University. The timing was both ironic and fitting. It had been exactly 100 years since the original crimson-and-black rugby-football team, with only three weeks' practice, had played and won its first game on a muddy field on the north side of the campus.

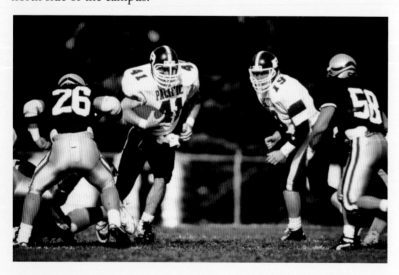

not seem so at the time. Of the $3.5 million that Pacific students received in aid in 1983, $2.5 million was from Federal sources.

If the university failed to comply with the guidelines of the Solomon Amendment, it faced the loss of all Federal support, a prospect it could ill afford. And while the college was not required to verify information reported on the compliance form, it was required to report to the Selective Service any information it had on file that contradicted what students entered on the forms.

It was to Pacific's and Duvall's credit that the university resisted the Solomon Amendment, which in effect discriminated against those who could not afford to attend college without financial assistance. The Financial Aid Office wrote several letters to Washington vigorously objecting to the new act, and Pacific University established a policy of continuing to provide non-Federal assistance to students who refused to sign the compliance form. These gestures did not go unnoticed by the students, and Duvall seemed to be off to a promising start.

WINS . . .

The '80s also witnessed the start of an unprecedented string of victories for Pacific on the athletic field.

Judy Sherman, coach of women's softball, remembers the early '80s as the most exciting time of her long career at Pacific (1967 to the present). Between 1980 and 1986 her teams stacked up an incredible six straight conference titles. In each of these years, the women Boxers advanced to the national play-offs, placing as high as third, and never lower than ninth, among the 16 top teams in the nation.

During these same years, under coach Tom Reynolds, the women's soccer team rounded out an impressive record of wins with two NAIA District II championships. The present-day soccer field on the Pacific campus is named after Reynolds.

In basketball, coach Bob Bonn led the men's team to NCIC conference titles in both 1986–87 and 1990–91, along the way racking up

the best career winning percentage of any coach in Pacific men's basketball history (NAIA Hall-of-Fame Coach Dan French, '56, holds the record for most wins). Under Coach Dave Olmstead, the women basketballers compiled an impressive 87 to 26 win-loss record, including a 40-game winning streak and four consecutive NCIC conference crowns between 1988 and 1992. For the 1990–91 season both Olmstead and Bonn were named Coaches of the Year in the Northwest Conference of Independent Colleges.

Even the Pacific football team, coming off a record-breaking string of 15 losing seasons, looked like a winner in 1988 when the Boxers set new team season records for passing yardage, passes attempted, and pass completions, and head coach Bill Griffin earned Coach of the Year honors from the league.

The fans who jammed McCready Field during that promising season could hardly have seen what lay just ahead for the football program at Pacific.

. . . AND LOSSES

Though Pacific athletics rode into the 1990s on the crest of victories, what many alumni remember most was the loss of football as a college sport. As might be expected at a school steeped in long traditions, this major break with the past did not go down easily.

Both the decision, and the process by which it had been arrived at, left hard feelings that, for some, continue to this day. The 1992 *Heart*

of Oak pointedly chose "Changing Traditions" as its theme, and uncharacteristically ran what amounted to an editorial. In an article entitled "Football Doesn't Score With The Board," the editor of the yearbook observed:

Many questions arose concerning the handling of the review process by the administration. A majority of those involved and affected by the cut, felt that the administration and key individuals involved, were not "playing fair," and that the decision to cut the program was already a "done deal" before it was released to the players, and the university community. President Duvall admitted to "false starts" made in informing the community and repeatedly apologized for the speed and manner in which the issue was handled …

This was neither the first nor last time that President Duvall's administrative manner would come into question.

A HOME FOR THE ARTS, A HOME FOR THE SCIENCES

While some may have questioned Duvall's style, few could deny that his contributions to life at Pacific were varied and significant—not least of all in the area of campus expansion. In this arena, at least, Duvall exhibited a good deal of diplomacy, simultaneously completing major additions to the facilities for both the arts and the sciences.

1993 saw the dedication of the Douglas C.

Left: Douglas C. Strain stands in front of the Science Center bearing his name.

Right: McCready Hall in the Taylor-Meade Performing Arts Center hosts a variety of performances every year.

Students stroll through Vandervelden Court, a 1995 addition to campus housing.

Strain Science Center, which is currently the home of the biology, computer science, math, and physics departments. The impressive, modern complex was named after Douglas Strain, founder of Electro Scientific Industries, and member of Pacific's Board of Trustees. The Strain family has had a long history with Pacific: Douglas Strain later served as chair of the board (1984–86) and his daughter Barbara, '70, has long been active in campus life generally, serving as president of Friends of Old College Hall and Friends of the Library, among others.

Also completed in the same year was the Taylor-Meade Performing Arts Center—named for Lucia Taylor, her daughter Gail Taylor-Meade, '70, and son-in-law Leon S.

Open to Debate: The Tom McCall Forum

NAMED IN HONOR of popular Governor Tom McCall, the first Tom McCall Forum was held in the Pacific University gymnasium in 1984 and featured William F. Buckley, Jr. and Senator Dick Clark. It and subsequent debates proved so successful that in 1992 the event was moved off-campus to the Portland Convention Center and then, in 1993, to its present sites, the Hilton Hotel for the banquet and the Arlene Schnitzer Concert Hall for the debate.

Over the years, the Tom McCall Forum has grown to become the premier public affairs event in Pacific's year, attracting more than 700 guests to the banquet alone from various corporate groups, and building funds for scholarships. Prominent pairings in the lively debates over the years have included Pat Schroeder and Jeane Kirkpatrick (1988), Judge Robert Bork and Arthur Schlesinger (1989), Jesse Jackson and Peter Ueberroth (1992), James Carville and William Safire (1995), and Dan Quayle and Robert F. Kennedy Jr. (1997).

Faculty members Seth Singleton (center) and Russ Dondero (right) listen to former vice president Dan Quayle at a question-and-answer session on campus before the 1997 Tom McCall Forum.

Meade, '70, long-time supporters of the arts on campus. The arts center contains the 400-seat McCready Auditorium and the Burlingham Recital Room. It also houses nine classrooms, six faculty offices, and enough room for two choral ensembles, three bands, and a full orchestra—a monumental improvement over the facilities available at Knight Hall, where the Music Department had been housed for many years.

Taylor-Meade Performing Arts Center provided long-overdue recognition of the importance of the music and theater programs at Pacific, both of which trace their origins back to the very beginning of the college. Two near-legendary figures in that long history include Frances Clapp, '08, who both studied and taught music at Pacific, and Charles Trombley, '52, who, besides being one of the most popular deans in the school's history, was famous on campus both as a vocalist and producer of musicals.

Finally, Duvall initiated the construction of Vandervelden Court, the new student apartments that were completed in the fall of 1995, shortly after Duvall left Pacific. The four complexes were named after Joe Vandervelden, '37, long-time Forest Grove businessman and resident, in gratitude for a future scholarship trust fund. Each apartment boasted four bedrooms, two bathrooms, a common kitchen, and a furnished living room, as well as such modern conveniences as a connection to the Internet and cable television. In all, the complex provided 142 tenants the student equivalent of luxury.

EXPANDING HORIZONS

Closer to Duvall's heart than expanding facilities, however, was expanding the horizons of Pacific beyond the confines of Forest Grove. The Tom McCall Forum is a good example. When Duvall arrived on campus in 1983, the debate series—then called the "Politics and Law Forum"—was a small-scale operation that had been initiated by Professor Russ Dondero and his students in the Political Science department. Beginning in 1981, the first two

Japan Day continues as an annual event at Pacific.

debates had been held in the University Center and attended mainly by other students. Approached by Dondero with the prospect of bringing Robert Kennedy, Jr. to campus, Duvall immediately saw the potential for turning the Forum into a major fund-raising event that would, at the same time, increase Pacific's visibility in the broader community. The plan was to combine the debate with a banquet and sell tables to corporate executives from the Portland metropolitan area. With this in mind, Dondero approached Audrey McCall to get permission to name the series after her late husband, Oregon's popular Governor Tom McCall.

Also significant in expanding Pacific's horizons was the founding, in 1988, of the Pacific Intercultural Institute and, to oversee and support it, the Pacific Intercultural Foundation. Initiated by Duvall and funded by a generous gift from the Matsushita Electric Companies of America and Japan, the institute built on and extended the historic ties between Pacific University and the Asia-Pacific region, particularly Japan. Its goal was to be a high-quality educational resource center not only for Pacific University students but for the state of Oregon and the entire Pacific Northwest.

Besides sponsoring various conferences, lectures, and teacher-exchange programs, the Pacific Intercultural Institute included an annual "Japan Day," during which high school students from throughout Oregon came to Pacific for the day and, communicating in Japanese, competed in sports, performed in skits, and learned more about the Japanese culture. While Japan Day continues as an annual event at Pacific, the institute itself ultimately proved financially unfeasible and, in 1992, was phased out in favor of the current Asian Studies program. Though short-lived, the Pacific Intercultural Institute played a significant role in raising local awareness about Asian relations. Today, thanks in part to teachers from Pacific University, Oregon leads the nation in the number of high schools that offer courses in the Japanese language.

These and other efforts went far toward putting Pacific on the Portland metropolitan map. When Duvall left Pacific in 1995, the school enjoyed a higher profile than at any time in its history. With only four years to its sesquicentennial anniversary and five to the millennium, Pacific University looked around for a leader who would take it into the 21st century.

Top right: Hawaiian students celebrate their graduation with masses of traditional flower leis.
Above: Students use the "Spirit Bench" to paint slogans and encouragement for various events.
Right: The Harvey Scott Memorial Library

The Pacific Century Campaign

$\mathcal{I}$N 1987, FOUR YEARS AFTER Bob Duvall came to the Pacific campus, the Board of Trustees decided to proceed with a capital campaign that would meet the physical needs of the campus, build endowment, and provide a stronger foundation for the university. With some trepidation, the Board agreed to the initial goal of $12 million over five years. When, after a fuller assessment of needs, the goal was raised to $18 million, everyone agreed this was going to be a real stretch. By 1989, when the campaign went public, the bar had been raised to $23 million.

The $23 million goal, if it could be met, would provide $3.9 million in added endowment, primarily for professorships and scholarships, $4.4 million for a new science facility, $4.6 million for an intercultural arts and music facility, $750,000 for the Harvey Scott Library, $1 million for scholarships and equipment for Optometry, $2.85 million for an intercultural institute, and $5.5 million for the Pacific Annual Fund and current academic programs.

Ben Whiteley

Early response to the campaign came mainly from long-time friends of Pacific. Prominent among the supporters were A. E. "Gene" Brim, who was appointed as head of the Campaign Steering Committee, and Ben Whiteley, who chaired the Board through part of this period. In 1988, trustee Jim Reynolds donated property to establish the Pacific Intercultural Institute, toward which Matsushita donated $1.5 million. Tom and Joyce Holce established an endowed chair in Science, later donating further money to an endowed Science scholarship; Eloise Bishop donated a major gift to the Music Building; and Lucia Taylor contributed substantially to the annual fund and to the Music Building. In 1989, Kathrin Cawein provided a gift of property to the campaign, and in 1990 Viola McCready Lasselle gave further trust funds to help with the Music Building campaign. Doug Strain, always one of Pacific's staunchest supporters, concentrated his efforts on the new science building (see page 119).

Tom Holce

As the campaign progressed, the foundation world stepped forward in a significant way, with the Meyer Memorial Trust providing $750,000 for the Optometry campaign and the Collins Foundation contributing $300,000 for the Music Building Fund and $400,000 for the Science Building. At the same time, Sequent Computer Systems provided a $1 million mainframe academic computer for the campus. The final year of the campaign was capped by the gift of $1 million from the M. J. Murdock Charitable Trust, monies from the Hall Templeton estate for the general endowment, and $261,000 from Willamette Industries.

When the capital campaign ended on September 15, 1993, President Duvall was able to announce that almost $25 million had been raised, an achievement that exceeded all expectations.

A.E. "Gene" Brim

The New Millennium: A New Beginning

We sustain ourselves in context, and the context is changing. This is the paradox of a learning organization. — FAITH GABELNICK, INAUGURAL ADDRESS, 1995

*A*LL GAIN involves an element of loss. As the 1995–96 school year approached, Pacific had gained considerable ground as a player in the broader community, but it had done so partly at the expense of morale on campus. A small but significant indicator of this shift was that the *Heart of Oak* had failed to appear for the past three years, the longest hiatus since the 1920s. It was no accident, therefore, that the new president, Faith Gabelnick, chose "community" and "connectedness" as two of the main themes of her new presidency, or that the internal issue to which she gave highest priority was "communication." After Gabelnick's first year, *Heart of Oak* returned.

A GOOD NOTE TO BEGIN ON

Nineteen-ninety-five was a year of divisiveness in America. It witnessed the tail end of the longest strike in baseball history, the bombing of a Federal building in Oklahoma City, the dismantling of affirmative action programs in California, the indictment of President Clinton's Whitewater business partners for fraud, the controversial acquittal of O.J. Simpson by a largely black jury, and the resignation of Oregon Senator Bob Packwood over charges of sexual harassment. With national trauma becoming somewhat routine, the mood of the country was more jaded than apprehensive.

At Pacific University, the mood was wait-and-see. President Duvall, never particularly visible on campus in recent years, had departed the scene altogether, and no one could predict what his successor might bring to a campus that was feeling out of touch with its leadership.

But if the Pacific community was apprehen-

In her formal academic robes, President Faith Gabelnick chats informally with Pacific alumni. A native of New York and raised in Connecticut, Gabelnick received her B.A. from Douglass College of Rutgers University, her M.A. in Literature from the University of Massachusetts, and her Ph.D. in Literary Studies from The American University in Washington, D.C. Before coming to Pacific, Gabelnick taught at The American University and the University of Maryland, and held administrative posts at Western Michigan University and Mills College. Gabelnick's administrative style as president is reflected in her many published writings and frequent lectures on stages of learning, curriculum development, and transformational leadership.

Elda Walker, '02, a noted botanist and long-time faculty member at the University of Nebraska, was the granddaughter of missionaries Elkanah and Mary Richardson Walker.

Frances Clapp, '08, served in the foreign missions in Japan.

sive about the arrival of its new leader in the person of Faith Gabelnick, its fears were soon allayed. For one thing, Gabelnick made a point of meeting with every campus constituency in the first few months, only after which did she deliver her first "state of the university" address to faculty, staff, and students. This approach reflected her background and training, which had been in the fields of community learning, organizational leadership, and systems thinking. With a reputation for educational change, she was eager to make it clear that change had to come from within, not be imposed from without. As she put it in an interview in the September 1995 *Index*: "I don't think an administrator or a president should be an isolated leader. I like the idea of servant leadership." The *Index* reporter noted of Gabelnick, "She believes it is important for the campus community to understand the decisions the president makes," adding that Gabelnick planned to hold open office hours for students every Thursday afternoon. "I'm going to be a presence on campus," Gabelnick asserted. Whether Gabelnick could make good on her promises was another matter, but the right note had been sounded, and people at Pacific were ready to give the new president a chance to deliver.

Fittingly, Gabelnick began her renovation by reviving an old Pacific tradition, Campus Beautification Day. In the spring of 1996, over 100 faculty, staff, and students rolled up their sleeves to plant flowers, trees, and bushes by way of appreciating and caring for their environment. The following summer saw the return of the outdoor concerts "Under the Oaks," a project long espoused by Performing Arts Director Paula Thatcher and finally funded during Gabelnick's term. Autumn witnessed the arrival on campus of the annual corn roast, which, in partnership with the Chamber of Commerce, continues to attract several thousand people each year. Also in the fall, Gabelnick extended Founders' Day to Founders' Week, bringing in speakers and special programs to celebrate Pacific's heritage. As

well, she set up monthly meetings with the mayor and city manager of Forest Grove to reinvigorate that historical connection. Both on campus and in the broader community, Pacific's first woman president was making her "presence" felt.

WOMEN AT PACIFIC: A RETROSPECT

While Faith Gabelnick is Pacific's first woman president, women have from the beginning played critical and often prominent roles in the school's history. Tualatin Academy and Pacific University, founded as they were by progressive Congregationalists, saw the education of women as an integral part of their mission. The original 1849 charter specifies "a Seminary of learning for the instruction of both sexes in science and literature." In 1881, Pacific's second president, Rev. John Herrick, had written: "Not to make ample provision for the education of women is to be behind the spirit of the age in which we live," adding that "the proper education of women has been recognized as an important, perhaps the chief factor of social progress." Such an attitude reflected, among other things, the Calvinist roots of the Congregationalist Church, by which women were considered a refining and beneficial influence on the crasser nature of the male sex, and therefore of society in general. As Rev. Herrick put it: "What is pure and modest and feminine in women, lies at the basis of our social purity and welfare."

But "social purity," whatever that might mean, had long since vanished as an ideal, and President Herrick's remarks are likely to strike modern ears as paternalistic at best. The fact remains, however, that Pacific University has always been ahead of the "spirit of the age" in its efforts to provide women with equal educational opportunities—this despite the predominance of male students during most of the college's history (1989–90 was the first year that women students outnumbered the men, a trend that has continued to the present).

Starting with Harriet Hoover Killin, Pacific's

first female graduate (1869), those efforts have provided the region and the nation with some of its finest elementary and high school teachers, as well as college professors such as Elda Walker '02, who became a noted botanist and long-time faculty member at the University of Nebraska. In the service professions generally, and especially in the foreign missions, female graduates of Pacific such as Frances Clapp '08, Nellie Walker '23, and Mary Ingle '33, contributed many decades of service in Japan, Hawaii, and elsewhere. And, closer to home, countless alumnae have always been the backbone of such organizations as the Friends of Old College Hall, the Friends of Music, and the Friends of the Library.

As for women among the faculty, we have singled out the beloved Mary Frances Farnham, but alumni from the '30s and '40s speak with equal respect of Gertrude Boyd Crane, who taught religion and philosophy, and whose blonde Pekinese, "Ah Sin," threatened to overthrow Boxer as a school mascot. In the College of Optometry, Dr. Anna Berliner, who taught at Pacific from 1949 to 1965, was a pioneer in establishing the close relationship between the behavioral sciences and the psychology of vision; in 1971 she received the American Optometric Association's prestigious Apollo Award for a lifetime of work that "deeply influenced the curriculum of every college of optometry." Women have served as the founding directors for the programs of physical therapy, occupational therapy and physician assistant studies. Outstanding women athletes such as Judy Sherman, athletic director, have brought honors to Pacific in regional and national arenas. During Gabelnick's term of office the number of tenured women faculty has increased significantly.

The Board of Trustees, too, though it has yet to appoint a woman as chairperson, has benefited over the years from the membership of senior board members such as Viola McCready, '31; Jean Tate, '52; Elizabeth Johnson; and Doris Burlingham.

The hiring of Faith Gabelnick, then, was

not so much a breaking with one tradition as the formal acknowledgment of another. The possibility of establishing a feminist studies program at Pacific had been in the air for some time, but no action had been taken. Then, in November 1995, 38 students signed a petition to the dean of Arts and Sciences requesting the development of such a program. The petition, which argued that feminist studies would offer a valuable alternative voice to the existing curriculum, coincided with the arrival

Dr. Anna Berliner

Above: Today the former library, Carnegie Hall, houses the School of Education, established in 1995.

Alumni Represent Oregon's First Congressional District

*T*WO PACIFIC University graduates have been elected in Oregon to seats in the United States Congress, both serving as representatives from Oregon's First District. Republican Thomas Tongue (1844–1903) completed his studies in 1868 and first went to Washington, D.C. in 1897. Graduating a century later, in 1969, Les AuCoin (1942–) became the first Democrat ever elected from the First District.

Thomas Tongue

Thomas Tongue, a native of England, practiced law in Hillsboro for many years. He served in the State Senate from 1888 to 1892 before successfully running for Congress. Tongue was elected to national office in 1896 and reelected three times. Unfortunately, his public service was cut short in 1903 when he died at the start of his fourth term. Rep. Tongue was personally responsible for Pacific's designation as Government Documents Repository #0504, only the third such designation in Oregon and a major boost for the library's collection.

Les AuCoin

Les AuCoin studied journalism, political science, and Biblical literature at Pacific. While finishing his bachelor's degree, he also worked as Pacific's director of public information. AuCoin began his political career in 1970 when he won a seat in the Oregon House of Representatives. Four years later, in 1974, he began an 18-year stint in Congress. AuCoin, a popular figure in the district, was reelected eight times. His service ended voluntarily when he gave up his seat to run unsuccessfully for the U.S. Senate against Bob Packwood. Pacific granted AuCoin an honorary doctor of letters degree in 1977, recognizing his contribution to the welfare of Oregonians statewide. Rep. AuCoin served on the Pacific University Board of Trustees from 1985 until 1998.

at Pacific of many new faculty already knowledgeable in this area. In response to the petition, a task force was formed to establish an outline of possible plans. The program received faculty approval in October of 1996, and the first course was offered in the following fall. The current Feminist Studies Program offers an interdisciplinary minor that investigates the significance of gender in all areas of human life.

CONNECTEDNESS

In choosing "connectedness" as the theme of her presidency, Gabelnick had her work cut out for her. In 1995, the year she arrived on campus, the university already had five graduate programs and was about to add a sixth. Most of these programs—optometry (1945), physical therapy (1975), occupational therapy (1984), and professional psychology (1985)—represented the only offerings in their respective fields in the state of Oregon—or, in the case of the O.D. degree in optometry and the Psy.D. degree in psychology, in the Pacific Northwest. The teacher education program that had been part of the College of Arts and Sciences at Pacific had been remodeled in 1994 to become the School of Education, which established one location on the Forest Grove campus and one in Eugene, adding yet other rooms to "the house that Marsh built."

All of these programs drew on the latest research in their particular disciplines and were practice-oriented, both in philosophy of approach and in the "hands-on" preparation of students. Importantly, the programs honored and extended the strong emphasis that the Congregationalist founders of Pacific University had placed on preparing professionals for service to the community. In many respects, however, the university acted as if it were simply a college of arts and sciences connected to an assortment of professional programs. The challenge would be to bridge the widening gap between the graduate professional programs and the liberal arts curricula that were supposed to constitute the core of Pacific University's identity.

In response to this challenge, Gabelnick established the Liberal Learning Task Force, made up of faculty from the College of Arts and Sciences and from the professional programs, to explore ways to link what, up to this point, had been separate and sometimes conflicting entities. As is often the case in family feuds, the various parties, when they sat down together and aired their respective agendas and grievances, found that they were not nearly as much at odds as they had for many years assumed. In particular, the task force found that a solid foundation in the liberal arts was as important to the professional programs as it was to the undergraduate programs, and that their respective curricula held many values and interests in common.

Out of the task force's discussions grew a proposal to the Hewlett Foundation of Menlo Park, California, for a three-year project to "explicitly connect and integrate our liberal arts and professional identities." In July of 1998, the Hewlett Foundation awarded Pacific University $375,000 to enable the faculty to rethink their curricula in partnership with their colleagues, and to develop collaborative teaching practices, particularly those that would bring the graduate and the undergraduate colleges together.

With the Hewlett Program entering its third year, the outcome of that effort remains to be seen, but the attempt itself is evidence that Pacific has not lost its flair for "acts of splendid audacity." Nor has it lost the dynamic tension between Sidney Harper Marsh's ideal that "The true aim of the scholar is truth and knowledge for its own sake" and the opposing view that preparation for professional careers is the more proper end of a university education. Rather than resolving these opposing views, Pacific University, as it enters the 21st century, seems almost comfortable in accepting them as complementary and integral parts of its unique identity.

Above: Quilters demonstrate their craft on Founders' Day, which started in 1993 as a Friends of Old College Hall event. Today Founders' Week culminates in the annual Founders' Day/Corn Roast, held on the campus in conjunction with the Forest Grove Chamber of Commerce. Right: President Gabelnick presides over the Hometown Hero Awards presented as part of Corn Roast.

Pacific Athletic Hall of Fame

*I*N 1993 PACIFIC established an Athletic Hall of Fame to honor graduates who have distinguished themselves on the athletic fields, or have played a "behind the scenes" rôle in supporting the athletic program.

Paul Stagg

Dick Daniels

Dan and Varina French

Nely Agbulos, Athlete, Softball, Volleyball, 1982

Susi Chaffee Armstrong, Athlete, Track & Field, Volleyball, 1979-83

Charles Bafaro, Coach, Baseball, 1963-94

Sally Baierski, Athlete, Softball, Soccer, 1985

Peaches Bode, Athlete, W-Basketball, Softball, 1982

Art Brachman, Athlete, Football, 1929-32

Frank Buckiewicz, Athlete, Football, Basketball, Baseball, Track, Golf, 1953, Coach, Football, Golf, 1965-80

Kris Chatari-Sanchez, Athlete, Volleyball, W-Basketball, 1977

Dr. Lund Chin, Athlete, M-Tennis, 1964

Mike Clock, Coach, Wrestling, 1967-88, 1991-92

Jim Corrigan, Athlete, Football, Basketball, Baseball, Track, 1936

Dick Daniels, Athlete, Football, Track & Field, 1968

Nancy Vanderwerf Edwards, Athlete, Softball, Volleyball, 1986

Deann Fitzgerald, Athlete, Softball, 1981

Roger Folgate, Coach, Football, 1936-42

Leo Frank, Coach, Football, 1921-29

Rick Franklin, Athlete, Wrestling, 1978

Dan French, Athlete, Football, Basketball, Track, 1956, Coach Basketball 1960-72

Varina French, Meritorious Service - PE Faculty, 1960-78

Lee Garboden, Athlete, Wrestling, 1971-75

Len Gilman, Athlete, Football, 1941

George Horner, Meritorious Service, 1944

Jean Horner, Meritorious Service, 1950s - 60s

Norm Hubert, Athlete, M-Basketball, 1955

Nancy Jewett, Athlete, Volleyball, Softball, 1972

Leon Johnson, Athlete, M-Basketball, 1964

Jack Killits, Athlete, M-Tennis, 1935

Bob Light, Athlete, Football, 1962

Lloyd Little, Athlete, Football, Baseball, 1975

Ruth Loomis, Meritorious Service, 1929-41

Gerald Millis, Athlete, Football, 1955

Dr. Cal Mosley, Athlete, Baseball, 1966

Doug Okabayashi, Athlete, Football, 1970, Meritorious Service

Vince Powell, Athlete, Baseball, 1968

Jana Ransom, Athlete, Softball, W-Basketball, Field Hockey, Track, 1975

Kelly Reed, Athlete, Softball, Volleyball, W-Basketball, 1982

Ed Ritt, Athlete, Wrestling, 1983

Harvey Roloff, Coach, M-Basketball, Football, 1946-56, 1941 Grad

Ed Rooney, Athlete, M-Basketball, Football, 1951

Stan Russell, Athlete, Football, 1950

Cindy Schuppert, Athlete, W-Basketball, Softball, 1983

Steve Sherrill, Athlete, Baseball, 1973

Brett Smith, Athlete, Football, 1985-87

Dan Spiering, Athlete, Football, Baseball, Booster Organizer, 1948

Paul Stagg, Coach, Football, 1947-60

Chris Tarabochia-Van Wagner, Athlete, W-Basketball, 1986

Arnold "Tug" Thorgenson, Athlete, Baseball, M-Basketball, Football, 1949

Kathy Thurman, Meritorious Service, 1976, 1980

Johanna Vaandering, Athlete, Softball, 1987

John Voorhies, Athlete, Baseball, 1968-72

Brenda Wall-Manser, Athlete, Softball, W-Basketball, 1980

GROUNDS FOR OPTIMISM

As this story of Pacific University is being written, President Faith Gabelnick has been at Pacific for only four years, but there has been progress on several fronts. The university has initiated two new master's programs, one in physician assistant studies and one in counseling, and is developing its third doctorate—this one in physical therapy. At the undergraduate level, thanks to a grant from the Murdock Trust, the university has launched a program of undergraduate research in the natural sciences. As for physical improvements, the College of Optometry has completed its "phase one" renovation of $3.5 million, and raised additional funds for classrooms equipped with the latest technology. Also, the university has hired a campus architect to embark on expanding the Pacific Athletic Center, renovate the University Center and the Library, and build special homes for School of Occupational Therapy, the School of Education, and the School of Professional Psychology.

These advancements have not gone unnoticed. The 1998 *U.S. New and World Report's* "Best-Value" edition ranked Pacific number one in Oregon for academic value, and third overall for value among comprehensive universities west of the Mississippi. What this translated to was national recognition that Pacific provided parents and students outstanding value for their education dollar. To the countless alumni who over the years had benefited from Pacific's abiding mission to provide quality education to students of limited means, this was hardly news.

Pacific has also witnessed major successes on the athletic field in the past four years. 1996 was especially good to the Boxers: for only the second time in the school's history, Pacific won three NCIC titles—in women's basketball, men's soccer, and golf. The women's basketball victory was especially exciting as the Boxers came from behind to upset the top-seeded Willamette University Bearcats, losers of only one game in the regular season, by a score of 66 to 55. In the following year Coach Ken

Schumann took the men's basketball team to the national play-offs for the first time in 63 years, and in 1998 Judy Sherman's softball squad won the NCIC championship for the first time since the remarkable six consecutive titles in the early 1980s.

Fittingly, 1998 also marked the 150th year since George Atkinson had ridden out on horseback from Oregon City to the West Tualatin Plains to see "what is called an orphan school" and had returned to record in his diary: "It is a good site and it may grow to some importance." Poised on the brink of the 21st century, the school built on that site could look back at Atkinson's words with satisfaction. Moreover, with an enrollment of 2,000 students, the highest in its history, taught by 160

Top: Freshmen sign the enrollment book in Old College Hall.
Above: The Index *Staff in the 1990s*

faculty who considered teaching their top priority, it could look to the future with optimism.

A GOOD NOTE TO END ON

Mark Twain once observed that as a teenager he considered his parents to be incurably dense, and that when he reached his twenties he was amazed by how much they had matured in so short a time. Children's perceptions of their parents are necessarily colored by a blissful ignorance of the challenges, financial and otherwise, that come with raising a family. Were this not the case, the only happy children would be those of wealthy parents.

This phenomenon applies as well to students' attitudes about their alma maters. There has hardly been a time in Pacific University's history when it has not been challenged by financial worries, and there has been more than one time when the university teetered on the brink of closure. And yet, with few exceptions, this is not what the alumni remember about their years at Pacific, if indeed they were even aware of it at the time.

Quite the contrary. What they remember, by and large, is the pervasive sense of security that the close-knit community of a small college provides. They remember the friendships, many of which are still strong, and the one-on-one interactions with a faculty member who was as concerned about their personal growth as their academic progress.

In her report to the Pacific community in 1997, Faith Gabelnick declared: "As we change, we must provide space for joy, play, and celebration. When we lose sight of the joy of learning, we undercut our mission and our core values." This is an appropriate note to end on, insofar as an ending is appropriate at all in the context of a school that has seemed, throughout its long history, to be forever on the verge of beginning anew.

The fact is, most institutions of Pacific University's age have become venerable, not to say stodgy. Pacific University has managed to remain young, with all the strengths and weaknesses attendant on that condition—a certain awkwardness about identity, perhaps, but coupled with an exhilarating sense that the best years still lie ahead. The challenges that face Pacific University's first woman president are hardly less daunting than those that faced its first male president 150 years ago. Some might find this grounds for discouragement; it is a mark of Pacific University's essential character to see it as a cause for celebration.

Appendices

Bibliography

The Pacific University Archives, located on the second floor of the Harvey W. Scott Memorial Library, contains much of the primary and secondary source material used in researching the book. Major holdings include manuscript collections (S.H. Marsh papers, Tabitha Brown letters, Pherne Brown Pringle Oregon Trail drawings, and others), Trustees' meeting minutes and committee reports, president's papers, financial reports, university publications (Bulletins and Catalogs, *Heart of Oak* yearbook, *Index* newspaper, *Pacific Today* and *Pacific* magazines, and others), biographical files, oral histories (audio and video tapes), alumni records, academic program reports, theses and dissertations (record copies), and historical photographs.

Anderson, Florence B. *Leaven for the Frontier: The True Story of a Pioneer Educator.* Boston: The Christopher Publishing House, 1953.

Brandt, Patricia, and Nancy Guilford, eds. *Oregon Biography Index.* Corvallis: Oregon State University (Kerr Library, Bibliographic Series No.11), 1976.

Buan, Carolyn. *A Changing Mission: The Story of a Pioneer Church.* Forest Grove, Oregon: The United Church of Christ (Congregational), 1995.

Carafiol, Peter. *Transcendent Reason: James Marsh and the Forms of Romantic Thought*, Florida State University Press, 1982

Carey, Charles Henry. *History of Oregon.* Three vols. Chicago: Pioneer Historical Publishing Co., 1922.

Clark, Robert D. *The Odyssey of Thomas Condon.* Portland: Oregon Historical Society Press, 1989.

Corning, Howard M., ed. *Dictionary of Oregon History.* Portland, Oregon: Binfords and Mort, Publishers, 1956.

Drury, Clifford M. *Nine Years with the Spokane Indians: The Diary, 1838-1848, of Elkanah Walker.* Glendale, California: The Arthur H. Clark Company, 1976.

Edwards, G. Thomas. *The Triumph of Tradition: The Emergence of Whitman College, 1859-1924.* Walla Walla (Washington): Whitman College, 1992.

Eells, Myron. *Biography of Rev. G.H. Atkinson, D.D.* Portland (Oregon): F.W. Baltes and Company, 1893.

Eells, Myron, ed. "A History of Tualatin Academy and Pacific University, Forest Grove, Oregon: 1848-1902." Unpublished typescript prepared for the Alumni Association, Pacific University, 1904.

Farnham, Mary F. "Who's Who Among the Alumni of Pacific, 1880-1930." Typescript, Pacific University Archives, n.d.

Forest Grove City Archives, Forest Grove, Oregon. City Ordinance, 1893.

Gaston, Joseph. *The Centennial History of Oregon, 1811-1912.* Four vols. Chicago: S.J. Clarke Publishing Co., 1912.

"George Henry Atkinson: A Pioneer Builder." *Pacific University Bulletin*, Vol. XL, No. 7 (June 1944). Reprinted in booklet form from *Pacific University Bulletin,* May 1944.

Gilbert, Alfred C. and Marshall McClintock. *The Man Who Lives in Paradise*. New York: Rinehart and Company, 1954.

Herrick, C. Judson. *George Ellett Coghill: Naturalist and Philosopher*. Chicago: University of Chicago Press, 1949.

Hitchman, James H. *Liberal Arts Colleges in Oregon and Washington, 1842-1980.* Bellingham, Washington: Center for Pacific Northwest Studies, Western Washington University, 1981.

Johansen, Dorothy O. and Charles M. Gates. *Empire of the Columbia.* 2nd ed. New York: Harper & Row, Publishers, 1967.

Johnston, Paul. "A Brief History of Pacific University." Typescript, Pacific University Archives, 1931.

Long, Watt A. "History of Pacific University." M.A. thesis, University of Oregon (Eugene), 1932.

McArthur, Lewis A. *Oregon Geographic Names*. 4th ed. Portland: Oregon Historical Society, 1974.

McCornack, Ellen Condon. *Thomas Condon: Pioneer Geologist of Oregon.* Eugene: University of Oregon Press, 1928.

Murie, Olaus J. "Wild Country as a National Asset." *The Living Wilderness,* Summer 1953.

Read, Richard T. "Institutionalizing Science in Oregon: The Role of the Oregon State Academy of Sciences, 1905-1914." Master's Thesis, Oregon State University, Corvallis, 1983.

Richardson, Steven W. "The Two Lives of John Smith Griffin." *Oregon Historical Quarterly*. Vol. 91, No. 4 (Winter 1990): 340-370.

Richardson, Robert. *Emerson, The Mind on Fire*, University of California Press, 1995.

Ritchie, M. A. F. *The College Presidency: Initiation into the Order of the Turtle.* New York: Philosophical Library, 1970.

Robertson, James R. "Origin of Pacific University." *The Quarterly of the Oregon Historical Society.* Vol. VI, No. 2 (June 1905): 109-146.

Schock, E.D. "A Comparative Study of the History of Representative Denominational Colleges and Universities in the Pacific Northwest." M.S. thesis, University of Idaho (Moscow), 1932.

Schoenberg, Wilfred P., S.J. *The Lapwai Mission Press.* Boise, Idaho: The Idaho Center for the Book, 1994.

Spooner, Ella Brown. *The Brown Family History.* Laurel, Montana: The Laurel Outlook, 1929.

Whitman College Archives, Walla Walla, Washington. Myron Eells Papers.

Williams, Edward F. *The Life of Dr. D.K. Pearsons, Friend of the Small College and of Missions.* New York: The Pilgrim Press, 1911.

Williams, George C. *Alanson Hinman: Pioneer of 1844.* Forest Grove (Oregon): George Williams, 1994.

Young, Judith and Celista Platz. *The Brown Family History II.* Newton, Kansas: Mennonite Press, 1992.

Board of Trustees: Presidents and Chairs

TERM	NAME
1848-1858	Rev. Harvey Clark
1858	Rev. Horace Lyman *(served April to September)*
1858-1859	Rev. Sidney Harper Marsh *(university president)*
1859-1862	Rev. Horace Lyman
1862-1865	Rev. Sidney Harper Marsh *(university president)*
1865-1866	Rev. Horace Lyman
1866-1875	Rev. Sidney Harper Marsh *(university president)*
1875-1878	Rev. Horace Lyman
1878-1879	Rev. Sidney Harper Marsh *(university president)*
1879-1890	Alanson Hinman
1890-1892	George Shindler
1892-1905	Alanson Hinman
1905-1910	Harvey Whitefield Scott
1910-1916	B.S. Huntington
1916-1922	Harrison G. Platt
1922-1924	W.J. McCready
1924-1926	H.E. Witham
1926-1935	B.S. Huntington
1935-1937	John F. Dobbs *(university president)*
1937-1945	Homer T. Shaver
1945-1953	Paul A. Davies
1953-1962*	George R. Rossman
1962-1970	Ronald M. McCreight
1970-1975	Charles K. Bishop
1975-1977	M. Vern Walker
1977-1980	Ralph Shumm
1980-1982	Al Bullier
1982-1984	Leland H. Johnson
1984-1986	Douglas C. Strain
1986-1991	Benjamin R. Whiteley
1991-1993	Thomas J. Holce
1993-1995	Howard L. Hubbard
1995-1998	A.E. "Gene" Brim
1999-	William H. Stoller

* Title changed from President to Chairman.

Pacific University Presidents

TERM	NAME
1854-1879	Sidney H. Marsh, D.D.
1879-1883	John R. Herrick, S.T.D.
1883-1891	Jacob F. Ellis, D.D.
1891-1900	Thomas McClelland, D.D.
1900-1913	William N. Ferrin, LL.D.
1913-1918	Charles J. Bushnell, Ph.D.
1919-1922	Robert F. Clark, L.H.D.
1922-1924	William C. Weir, M.S.
1924-1940	John F. Dobbs, LL.D.
1941-1953	Walter C. Giersbach, B.D. (etc.)
1953-1958	Charles J. Armstrong, Ph.D. (etc.)
1959-1970	Miller A.F. Ritchie, L.H.D. (etc.)
1970-1983	James V. Miller, B.D. (etc.)
1983-1995	Robert F. Duvall, Ph.D.
1995-	Faith Gabelnick, Ph.D.

Photograph Credits

All photographs are from the Pacific University Archives or other University collections unless otherwise noted below.

Page	Credit
4	Ivy: Robert Graves
7	Sesquicentennial Quilt: Woodrow Blettel
9	Gary Miranda and Rick Read: Woodrow Blettel
11	Old College Hall: Woodrow Blettel
12	Tree trunk: Woodrow Blettel
14	Whitman Mission site: Oregon Historical Society Field Services Program
15	Harvey Clark: Forest Grove United Church of Christ Archives
15	Champoeg State Park obelisk: Woodrow Blettel
20	Tree: Woodrow Blettel
22	George Atkinson and family: Forest Grove United Church of Christ Archives
23	Charter: Oregon State Archives #2817
28	James Marsh: Bailey/Howe Library, University of Vermont
35	Walker Hall and Knight Hall: Woodrow Blettel
39	University Falls: Washington County Historical Society
42	Porch posts, Knight Hall: Woodrow Blettel
44	J. R. Herrick: University of South Dakota Archives
45	Freshman in library: Oregon Historical Society, #399, OrHi 10130
46	General O. O. Howard: Oregon Historical Society #529, OrHi 38308
47	Horace Lyman: Forest Grove United Church of Christ Archives
47	Alanson Hinman: Forest Grove United Church of Christ Archives
49	Indian Training School Uniform button loaned courtesy George Fox University Library; photograph by Woodrow Blettel
50	Corner of Marsh Hall: Woodrow Blettel
52	Steps of Marsh Hall: Robert Graves
57	Music class: Robert Graves
62	D.K. Pearsons: from The Life of Dr. D. K. Pearsons, Friend of the Small College and of Missions by Edward Franklin Williams, The Pilgrim Press, 1911
63	Henry Winslow Corbett: Oregon Historical Society #284, OrHi74121
66	Trombley Square: Woodrow Blettel
69	"Prin" Bates: Oregon Historical Society, OrHi78840
73	Titanic lifeboat: National Archives and Records Administration, NRAN-21-SDNYCIVCAS-55(279)-I

Museum artifacts on pages 17, 18, 19, 22, 45, 49, 56, 62, 69, 78, 81, 87, and 118 were photographed by Woodrow Blettel.

Index

Page numbers in *italics* indicate photographs and/or captions